GW00994545

VISION
OF
GLORY

An exposition of the Book of Revelation

WILLIAM STILL

Also in the Didasko series:
Towards Spiritual Maturity: William Still
Lord From The Depths I Cry (Job): George Philip
The Power of God (Romans): James Philip

First edition published 1987
by Nicholas Gray Publishing
26 Bothwell Street,
Glasgow G2 6PA

ISBN 0 948643 03 X

Typeset by: Nuprint Ltd, Harpenden, Herts AL5 4SE
Printed by Bell and Bain Ltd, Glasgow

Contents

Introduction to Didasko

One of the constant needs of the church, and a reiterated appeal from individual Christians today, is for *biblical teaching*. Does the Bible carry a message from God which speaks to us with relevance and power in these closing years of the twentieth century? Does it have something to say which will have practical repercussions in the lives of men and women and young people? If so, our first priority must be to grasp its message. The aim of the *Didasko* series of books is to meet this need through exposition of the books and fundamental doctrines of the Bible. *Didasko* is the New Testament's word for 'I teach'. We know from the New Testament that the basic element in the early church's teaching was the exposition of the Scriptures in a way that was clear, lively and Christ-centred. Precisely this is the purpose of all the writers who will share in this series of books.

Most, but not all, of the books in the *Didasko* Series are in the form of straightforward biblical exposition. They are not technical commentaries. Rather they explain the meaning of the biblical text and provide application of it to the Christian life. The contributors to this series are mainly men with considerable personal Christian experience and years of pastoral experience working with and helping Christians to understand the gospel more fully and to live in obedience to it.

It is the conviction of the publisher, contributors and the general editor of the *Didasko* Series that there is a great need for the kind of literature which this series represents. Their hope is that these books will contribute to meeting that need and will give instruction, challenge and encouragement to Christians thoughout the world.

SINCLAIR B. FERGUSON
Series Editor

Acknowledgements

This study in the Book of Revelation began with several series of sermon and Bible Study notes. It was given considerable impetus when I was asked to expound the entire book of Revelation at the Scottish Conference of the Inter-Varsity Fellowship (now UCCF) at St Andrews in March, 1971.

After much study of Revelation, I still find that considerable mystery remains, and some of my comments are but interim reflections on an inexhaustible theme. Now, having revised the text following a series of sermons delivered in 1982-83, I still draw heavily on *More than Conquerors* by William Hendriksen, and gladly acknowledge his help in understanding the structure of the book and its glorious message. The text used is that of the Revised Standard Version.

I am grateful to Mrs Eleanor Leslie for many hours spent in reviewing the text and in rooting out errors and crudities; and I thank my friend James Philip, and some of our editing team for useful suggestions.

Foreword

A vision of glory

Many Christians think of the Book of Revelation as the most mysterious and difficult book in the entire Bible. John Calvin, when asked why he had written studies on every other part of the New Testament but never on Revelation, is reputed to have replied that he did not understand it. That may be a comfort to us! Indeed, one of the things that can prevent us from studying Revelation is that we have been discouraged by people who are certain they understand it!—often in such detail that they can identify the contemporary events about which (in their opinion) Revelation speaks.

Sometimes our basic problem is a failure to grasp the kind of book Revelation is intended to be. We read it as 'history written before its time'. But in fact Revelation is more of a picture-book than a history text-book. It is a tapestry full of symbols conveying essentially one great message; it is a kind of divine stained-glass window through which we are meant to see what Paul calls, literally, 'the multi-coloured wisdom of God' (Eph. 3:10). Each picture which Revelation sets before us is meant to lead us to an ever deeper conviction that our God reigns, and that Jesus Christ really is Lord.

Paradoxically, it is often youngsters who grasp this more easily than adults. I speak from personal experience, for I remember one winter Saturday in my early teens spending my entire pocket money to buy a paperback edition of J. B. Phillips' translation of Revelation (it cost two shillings and

11

six pence, in what my children patronisingly think of as the 'old days'!). The experience of sitting beside a warm fire that Saturday afternoon and reading Revelation from start to finish was one I shall never forget. So vivid and full of power did the pictures seem that I felt I could almost see and hear what John was describing in his vision. Uncluttered by speculation about the meaning of the book's details, its message seemed as clear as it must have done to those first hard-pressed Christians who received it: The Lord reigns!

No one can expound Revelation properly who does not 'see' its pictures. In this respect William Still is well qualified. Not only has he preached through the entire book of Revelation on some four different occasions, and twice written study notes on it for his congregation, but he has a profound appreciation (indeed, enjoyment) of visual imagery. It is clear in these pages that he shares with John a sense of excitement and joy in the way Christ unveils His glory in this vision.

Here, in *A Vision of Glory,* William Still takes us 'behind the scenes', explaining Scripture patiently and practically. In doing so he also leads us into the message of the Book of Revelation, in which Christ Himself takes us 'behind the scenes' of history to show us its real meaning and its ultimate destiny. William Still's exposition will open up what for many Bible readers has been not so much a revelation as a closed book. And it will do so principally because its author is conscious throughout that the book is intended to be a *revelation of Jesus Christ Himself.*

SINCLAIR B. FERGUSON
Westminster Theological Seminary,
Philadelphia, U.S.A.

Introduction

The Greek for 'revelation' is *apocalypse,* from the verb *apocalupto,* I unveil. The *Apocalypse,* therefore, is the unveiling by God the Father, of his Son Jesus Christ. This is a remarkable use of the word 'revelation', since the book is full of mystery; but it is, none the less, revelation in mystery, for in it Jesus Christ is portrayed in all the glory of His Person and work as eternal Son, eternal Man and eternal King and Saviour.

The book belongs to a class of ancient literature called Apocalyptic, which flourished during the two centuries before, and the century after Christ. Its nature is, generally, a heavenly message to a man of God, usually to afford comfort, and to give hope of divine intervention to the Lord's people in time of tribulation and persecution: 'It purported to bring revelation from God explaining the reason for the prevalence of evil, disclosing heavenly secrets, and promising the imminent coming of His kingdom and the salvation of the afflicted.' (G. E. Ladd, *The New Bible Dictionary,* p.43).

Apocalyptic literature arose after the time of the post-exilic prophets, Haggai, Zechariah and Malachi, when God no longer spoke to his people through a living voice. The times were exceedingly and increasingly evil. Men longed for the Messiah to appear, but there was nothing but oppression for the long-suffering Jews (especially in the days of Antiochus Epiphanes, *c*168 BC).

13

To try to 'fill this vacuum', apocalyptic literature appeared, purporting to speak from God. Two of these apocalyptic works are in the Apocrypha, 2 Esdras and Apocalypse of Baruch. Other apocalyptic works include the first and second books of Enoch (see Jude 14, 15), Jubilees, Assumption of Moses and the Psalms of Solomon. Ladd summarizes the nature of Apocalyptic in five points: (1) Revelatory; (2) Imitative; (3) Pseudonymous (purporting to be by famous prophets; either by their disciples seeking to perpetuate their teaching, or disingenuously using their names to authenticate their message, or even to make their literature 'sell'!); (4) Symbolic; (5) Pseudo-predictive. (See *The New Bible Dictionary,* pp.43, 44).

In fact, Apocalyptic literature was largely spurious, for history was written as if it were predictive prophecy. It is clear, therefore, why scholars were tempted, faced with fictitious works, to assume that *all such literature* was false. Some scholarship has been so influenced by extra-biblical literature, that it has read biblical literature in the 'light' of contemporary pagan literature, not by way of interesting commentary, which is fair enough, but rather as regulative and determinative of the value to be set upon biblical literature. No one who believes the Bible to be the Word of God, and who believes that God inspired earlier scholars and saints to select the sacred canon of Scripture unerringly, can possibly accept such a viewpoint. In any case, the conscience of every thoughtful Christian is at liberty to judge the categorical worth of these works against the sacred Scriptures.

The characteristic spirit of apocalyptic literature can be summarized in four categories:

(1) *Dualistic:* it sets the coming age as wholly good over against the present age as bad, and that in a non-eschatological [non-final] sense: that is to say, it promises a this-worldly paradise in merely natural terms.

(2) *Deterministic*, or fatalistic.

(3) *Pessimistic*. The corollary of its being Dualistic was that it had no hope for the present age.

(4) *Ethically Passive*. It lacked moral incentives.

There is, of course, a clear and categorical difference

between that literature in general, and *biblical* apocalyptic literature in particular, such as Joel, Daniel, Ezekiel and Zechariah.

As to the author of Revelation, it would not be profitable here to enter into lengthy discussion on the authorship of the book, or of the Johannine literature in general. One or two quotations will suffice, and should prove helpful. Leon Morris quotes R. A. Edwards: 'The fact from which we start is that antiquity assigned the whole of Johannine literature to one man' (the Gospel, the Epistles, and the Revelation). 'That judgment,' says Edwards, 'ought only to be disturbed on irrefutable grounds' (L. Morris, Commentary on Revelation, I.V.P., 1971, p.33).

Donald Guthrie, writing on the book of Revelation, remarks, 'So strong is this evidence that it is difficult to believe that they (the ancient authors) all made a mistake in confusing the John of the Apocalypse with John the apostle.... It must be conceded that taken as a whole it (the evidence) points very strongly to the probability that the John of the Apocalypse was, in fact, John the apostle.' (*New Testament Introduction,* 1970, p.935).

In a similar vein, Professor T. F. Torrance writes: 'In regard to the difficult question of authorship, examination of the evidence makes it more and more difficult to hold that this John was not John the disciple of Jesus.' (*The Apocalypse Today,* p.6).

There was no dissent with regard to the authorship of the book until the time of Dionysius (died AD 264), which is fairly late. The date of the book of Revelation, as far as we can determine, was very likely in the time of the Emperor Domitian, successor to Nero (and like him too!), AD 90–95.

As to the book itself, and its interpretation, may God help us! No one can expect his interpretation of Revelation to be universally accepted. We can only glance at the main types of interpretation. There are several schools of thought.

There is the *Preterist* view, which regards the book as dealing *only* with the first century, its own time.

There is the *Historicist* view, which sees the book of Revelation as forecasting the whole of human history. (There is more divergence within this view than elsewhere; there are various Historicist views.)

Then there is the Futurist view, which holds that after the third chapter, all is future, pointing to the end of the age and dealing with things *only* at the end of the age, not at any other time.

There is the Idealist view, which regards the book generally, not as of events, but as of ideals, principles and doctrines poetically and apocalyptically expressed.

There is a sense in which we need all these views. The Preterist is relevant to the first and early second centuries, providing a history of these times. The Historicist points beyond the day in which it was written, right through to our day, and beyond, to the end. The Futurist is, of course, an element in the Historicist's view. As to the Idealist, the Revelation is certainly full of doctrine, but it is doctrine whose principles are wrought out in time, in the prophetic past, present and future. It is called the book of prophecy. Especially in the last chapter, 'prophecy' is mentioned a number of times.

As to the source of these studies in the Revelation, beyond the Scriptures themselves I have used as principal guide, William Hendriksen's *More than Conquerors*; but I have also used Leon Morris' *Tyndale Commentary,* Professor Thomas F. Torrance's *The Apocalypse Today,* R. H. Charles in *The International Critical Commentary* series, and many other books, including a number on the seven churches of chapters 2 and 3, especially that by Professor E. M. Blaiklock: also the modern post-millenial study, *An Eschatology of Victory,* by J. Marcellus Kik.

Hendriksen views the book as divided into seven sections (the perfect number); chapters 1–3; 4–7; 8–11; 12–14, 15–16; 17–19; 20–22. This view has a long and honourable history. Hendriksen cites Augustine, Cocceius and Hengstenberg among others who held it, while Leon Morris notes that Victorinus of Pettan (3rd cent. AD) regarded the repetition of the sevenfold judgments as part of the author's methods. However G. T. Manley urges the reader to maintain 'an open mind to deal with each portion of the book....' Morris calls this 'good advice.' Nonetheless, B. B. Warfield stands by the sevenfold division of the book, citing Ewald,

Weiss and Farrar (among others) in support. There are only two differences between Hendriksen's divisions of the Revelation (beyond separating both a Prologue and Epilogue) and Warfield's. Warfield continues the second section (chs. 4–7) into 8:1; and he ends the sixth division (chs. 17–19) at 19:10, the seventh section commencing at 19:11.

Hendriksen lays the seven sections one on top of the other, each division covering the same span of time, namely between the first and second comings of Christ. This span of history is therefore covered seven times in different expansions and emphases, with, of course, a mounting climax of both judgment and blessing towards the last section. This ingenious arrangement may seem artificial at first, but having perused Hendriksen with increasing care for twenty years, and having used his interpretation increasingly during that period, I have no hesitation in saying that the whole scheme in its all-embracing simplicity becomes more and more acceptable and illuminating, especially, be it noted, since the climax of the sections (chapters 3, 7, 11, 14, 16, 19, 21, 22) seems to fit the end of the age.

CHAPTER ONE

Jesus Christ Revealed
1:1-20

¹The revelation of Jesus Christ, which God gave him to show to his servants what must soon take place; and he made it known by sending his angel to his servant John, ²who bore witness to the revealed word of God and to the testimony of Jesus Christ, even to all that he saw.

The revelation is the unveiling of Jesus Christ (contrast the words of Charles Wesley's Christmas hymn, 'Veiled in flesh the God head see'; in Revelation we have the unveiling of Jesus Christ in power and glory), which God authorised and gave to his Son in order that he by the Spirit might show to His servants (John is *His servant*) what must soon take place.

Note the sequence of persons involved in the transmission of the Revelation: God the Father; the Son, Jesus Christ; the angels speaking to John (*cf* the mediation of angels in the giving of the Law at Sinai, Acts 7:38, 53; Gal. 3:19; Heb. 2:2); then those reading the Revelation, enabling others to hear and receive it. That is how the Word is handed down, by such steps, until it reaches us.

What does 'what must soon take place' mean? Torrance says about 'soon' and 'late' and the early coming of our Lord, 'The New Testament does not think of the difference between the presence of Christ here and now, and His Second Advent so much in terms of a passage of time as the difference between the veiled and the unveiled. That is why the whole New Testament by an inner necessity of personal faith

19

thinks of that day as imminent.' It is, of course, when we are living close to Him that we feel the imminence of His coming. This must be why particularly devoted saints have felt so sure that the Lord was coming soon.

It is sometimes said that the New Testament writers were 'mistaken' concerning Christ's early coming; but surely 'mistaken' is not a proper word to use about this profound sense of the imminence of the Lord's coming. Paul certainly longed for Christ to come before he died and, for that reason, in 2 Corinthians 5:1–10 he ignores the intermediate state between mortal body and immortal body, although he recognised the fact of such a state earlier in both 1 Thessalonians 4:13–17 and 1 Corinthians 15:51. Was not a sense of the imminence of the Lord's coming an inevitable effect of a sense of His spiritual nearness?

Soon? Listen to Peter: 'Do not ignore this one fact, beloved, that with the Lord one day is as a thousand years, and a thousand years as one day.' Even now it is less than two 'days' since the Lord came! 'The Lord is not slow about his promise as some count slowness, but is forbearing toward you, not wishing that any should perish, but that all should reach repentance.' (2 Pet. 3:8,9).

This testimony to which John bore witness, is of Jesus Christ. He, in His Person, work, and as Head over all, is the testimony. Christ *is* the Revelation which the Father gives to us and which we see so gloriously in this book.

³*Blessed is he who reads aloud,* in public, *the words of the prophecy,* see the word 'prophecy' mentioned frequently in chapter 22:6, 7, 9, 10, 16, 18, 19, *and blessed are those who hear, and who keep what is written therein*; there are seven 'beatitudes' in the book: the first here, the others in 14:13; 16:15; 19:9; 20:6; 22:7, 14; *for the time is near.*

The last days began with Christ, since He is God's last Word to man (Heb. 1:2). No one knows how long they will go on, but those who see time shot through with eternity, and God's eternal purposes threaded through all, can certainly see and feel the notion of one day as a thousand years and as one day. Note that the blessing is to those who read, hear, and *keep* the words: reading and hearing are not enough. If the Word does not affect how we live, it has not been received as the life-transforming power it is.

⁴*John to the seven churches that are in Asia*: there were more than seven churches (note the perfect number) in that area, including Colosse and Hierapolis. There are three Asias; the continent, the country (Asia Minor, which we now call Turkey), and the province or county. This is the county, with Ephesus the capital, where Paul preached for more than three years, and whence the gospel went out: 'All Asia heard the Word.' (Acts 19:10)

Grace to you and peace from him who is and who was and who is to come, this is not the Trinity, Father, Son and Holy Spirit, but rather the Godhead in threefold reference, *and from the seven spirits who are before his throne*, There is only one Holy Spirit: the perfect number seven reflects the fulness and perfection of the Spirit's Person and the manifoldness of His working, or 'charismata'. See also the same expression in 3:1; 4:5; 5:6.

⁵*and from Jesus Christ the faithful witness*, Jesus Christ is the only perfectly faithful witness to the Father (Heb. 1: 1, 2). 'For he whom God has sent utters the words of God, for it is not by measure that he gives the Spirit (to Him); the Father loves the Son, and has given all things into his hand.' (John 3:34, 35). Christ alone has monopoly of the gifts of the Spirit, since He has not only the fulness of the Person of the Spirit but the full range of the Spirit's charismata or gifts (Is. 11:2, 3). Not so we: we have the Person, but only a distribution of the gifts of the Spirit, and each bestowed only in measure (Rom. 12:3b; Eph. 4:7). Indeed, it takes the whole local church to contain and exercise a full range of the gifts, and the whole church in all ages to embrace them fully. *the first-born of* [from] *the dead,* see Romans 8:29; Colossians 1:18; Hebrews 2:10, 11. Christ in His resurrection is the first of the new order of indestructible manhood and, in the sense of being the first Man to pass through mortal life and death emerging into immortal Manhood, He is the pioneer, or file-leader, or path-finder. Because He has gone through, we shall go through after Him, see Hebrews 12:1, 2. *and the ruler of kings on earth.* He is King of Kings and Lord of lords, see Revelation 17:14; 19:16. In virtue of His victory over all created powers, angelic and human, signified

22   *A Vision of Glory*

by His ascension, exaltation and enthronement, He is
Prophet (Witness), Priest (Firstborn from the dead), King
(Ruler).

To him who loves us, actually 'loving us', an eternal fact
(Jer. 31:3), *and freed us from our sins by his blood',* one
letter in the Greek raises the question whether the word
means 'freed' (loosed) or 'washed'. Although most modern
translators prefer 'freed', the idea of 'washed' cannot be
denied as a possibility since it is found in Revelation 7:14.
Charles *(The International Critical Commentary)* associates
it with water references in Exodus, *eg* 19:10, 14. See also
Isaiah 1:18; 1 Corinthians 6:11; Hebrews 9:14. But 'freed' is
perhaps better here. *⁶and made us a kingdom,* not kings as
in AV (KJV). We are royal and divine but not *Deus* (God),
although Jesus, quoting Psalm 82:6 in John 10:34, speaks of
us as 'gods'. That extreme statement is to be taken in the
context of our partaking of the divine nature (2 Pet. 1:4), but
not of the Godhead. *priests to his God and Father,* here are
suggested the royal and priestly tribes, Judah and Levi, as
applied to our Lord and to us; for although our Lord was not
of the priestly tribe according to the flesh, yet He is our great
High Priest (Heb. 4:14–16), and we are priests after Him in
Peter's sense when he bids us be 'like living stones, built
into a spiritual house, to be a holy priesthood to offer
spiritual sacrifices acceptable to God through our Lord Jesus
Christ.' (1 Pet. 2:5) See this idea again in Revelation 5:10.

... to him be glory and dominion for ever and ever. Amen. It
is a fact seldom mentioned that the Son will hand over His
kingdom to His Father when it is completed. The clearest
reference to this is in 1 Corinthians 15:24, 25, but the 'until'
there, quoted from Psalm 110:1, is frequently quoted in the
New Testament. The submission of the Son to the Father
from all eternity, through time, to all eternity, is one of the
deepest and highest wonders of the mystery of the Godhead.

⁷Behold, he is coming with the clouds, of glory (see Mtt.
24:30), *and every eye will see him,* these words with Matthew
24:29–31 indicate the cosmic nature of the coming, *every
one, who pierced him*; see Zechariah 12:10 for the origin of
this expression; *and all tribes of the earth will wail on account
of him. Even so. Amen.* See Revelation 6:15–17. This is the

beginning of the final reckoning when men see Who it is they have rejected. We have a faint notion of how terrible that will be in Saul of Tarsus' shock when, on the road to Damascus he learned that Jesus of Nazareth, whom he despised, was addressing him from heaven's glory.

[8]*'I am the Alpha and the Omega,' says the Lord God, who is and who was and who is to come, the Almighty.* Alpha and Omega are the first and last letters of the Greek alphabet. This idea is given simpler expression in verse 17, and both expressions are given in 21:6, and even more fully in 22:13. It is difficult to get away from the solemn implication that here the Lord Jesus Christ is speaking as, and from, the Godhead. No more exalted ground could be taken.

[9]*'I, John, your brother',* This is the beginning of the vision, and is introductory to it, giving the occasion (vv.9–11). John puts himself on our level. Astonishingly, there is no claim to special authority; the facts proclaim it, as they often do—a lesson in humility for us, who will never range apostolically high like him. *who share with you in Jesus,* a fine expression of the activity of brotherhood, *the tribulation and the kingdom and the patient endurance,* see how beautifully 'kingdom' is set between 'tribulation' and 'patient endurance'. It is the light of the knowledge of the kingdom which gives glory to the darkness of the tribulation and endurance of suffering (see Col. 1:24; Phil. 3:10; 2 Cor. 4:7–12). There is nothing morbid here; all has a healthy purpose: see Hebrews 12:2, 'Who for the joy that was set before him endured the cross, despising the shame, and is seated at the right hand of the throne of God.' *was on the island called Patmos,* an island of the Dodecanese, four by eight miles in size, of black stone painfully quarried by slave and prison labour—a desolate place, *on account of the word of God and the testimony of Jesus.*

Hendriksen asks whether John was there because 'he refused to drop incense upon the altar of a pagan priest as a token of worshipping the emperor.' 'We are not sure,' he says (*More than Conquerors,* pp.69, 70) but we know that John preferred loyalty to the Lord he loved to that of any other competitor. Here it would seem that the incarnation of Jesus Christ and all testimony to it, including the prophetic, are bound together as one, so that modern attempts to separate Christ from the written record and revelation of the Word of God for the purpose of avoiding charges of errancy are naughty and mischievous.

[10]*I was in the Spirit,* this can mean nothing less than that John was taken over by the Spirit and elevated, in what we might regard as a trance state, to a high degree of spiritual sensitivity and reception, leading to divine insight into the holy mysteries of God (*cf* Daniel chapter 10) *on the Lord's day,* which became the Christian Sabbath commemorating the resurrection of Christ on the first day of the week; see John 20:19; Acts 20:7a; 1 Corinthians 16:2; *and I heard behind me a loud voice like a trumpet,* as of old the trumpet commands attention; see Exodus 19:16, 19; Leviticus 25:9; Joshua 6:5; Isaiah 58:1; Joel 2:1; Zechariah 9:14; 1 Corinthians 15:52.

[11]*saying, 'Write what you see in a book and send it to the seven churches, to Ephesus and to Smyrna and to Pergamum and to Thyatira and to Sardis and to Philadelphia and to Laodicea.'* To understand chapters 1 to 3, a Bible map is helpful to show the location of these cities in the Roman province of Asia. Ephesus was the centre of Paul's preaching for three years, whence the gospel went out to all the province, which led to the founding of churches, such as Colosse which Paul had never visited.

[12]*Then I turned to see the voice that was speaking to me,* it was the possessor of the voice he turned to see, *and on turning I saw seven golden lampstands,* corresponding to the seven churches, [13]*and in the midst of the lampstands one like the son of man,* This expression is first found in Daniel 7:13: the Son of Man is always in the midst of His people. Hebrews 2:10–18 portrays the Son of Man as our (elder) Brother leading the other (junior) sons to glory. In a quotation from Psalm 22:22 he states His intention to declare God's name prophetically to His brothers and to stand among them singing praise with them to the Father, the Lord inhabiting or being enthroned on the praises of Israel, Ps. 22:3. We need to take this seriously and imaginatively when we join in worship, seeing the Lord Jesus Christ standing invisibly in the midst, singing His heart out to His Father louder than

any! 'Where two or three are gathered in my name, there am I in the midst of them.' (Matt. 18:20) *clothed with a long robe,* speaking of dignity, *and with a golden girdle round his breast*; the gold speaking of deity, see Daniel 10:5.

God of Deity

[14]*his head and his hair were white as white wool, white as snow* (Is. 1:18); does this not speak of the dazzling brightness of the pure mind and heart of God? *his eyes were like a flame of fire* (Dan. 10:6b), the penetration of the all-seeing eye (see Ps. 139); or think of Hagar in her plight: 'Thou God seest me' (Gen. 16:13); or Jesus as the Light of the world, exposing men's evil deeds (John 3:17–21); [15]*his feet were like burnished bronze, refined as in a furnace,* surely the glory of the purposeful motion of His will, *and his voice was like the sound of many waters* (Dan. 10:6; Ezek. 43:2); we think of the thunderings of Sinai (Exod. 19:16; 20:18), or of Victoria Falls ('the smoke that thundered,' the Africans called it), or Niagara, an overwhelming aural experience; [16]*in his right hand he held seven stars* (explanation later), *from his mouth issued a sharp two-edged sword,* see Isaiah 11:4; 49:2; 2 Thessalonians 2:8; Hebrews 4:12. Do the two cutting edges of the short Roman sword, tongue-like in shape, suggest two sorts of judgment, of His own and of His enemies? Or universal judgment? *and his face was like the sun shining in full strength.* See Ezekiel 43:2; Matthew 13:43; Paul on the road to Damascus (Acts chapters 9:22, 26); Revelation 10:1; 20:11. How fearful and wonderful to think that the God of all judgment (the book of the Revelation is a book of judgment) has a face, and is personal (that is, He knows and cares), and is all-glorious.

[17]*When I saw him, I fell at his feet as though dead.* Compare the awe of Moses at the burning bush (Exod. 3), Isaiah in his vision (Isa. 6), Daniel in the visitation by the angel (Dan. 10), Paul in his humbling encounter on the road to Damascus (Acts 9), and in his ecstatic experience (2 Cor. 12); and consider the striking contrast between John, the beloved disciple, leaning on Jesus' breast (John 13:25; 21:20), and prostrate in a trance before the same Christ in glory. Could there be a greater extreme than these two experiences?

But he laid his right hand upon me, saying, 'Fear not, He is the same kindly Christ as cherished His young disciple in

His earthly days. This is always His word to those who submit to Him: 'Fear not!' *I am the first and the last,* see Isaiah 44:6; 48:12 for the source of this phrase, [18]*and the living one;* He is not only the One who is from eternity to eternity, but He is the ever-living One from first to last. None the less, *I died,* the eternal One has known mortal death, *and behold I am alive for evermore*; but having died a mortal death and having been raised from it by God, the fruit of that experience is gained for ever, and the immortal life gained is one that preserves that fruit for further purposes of death and resurrection in us; see Romans 6:9; Acts 2:27 (Psa. 16); Acts 2:31; *and I have the keys of Death and Hades.'* This means that the souls of the righteous are now with Christ, and although their bodies are held in mortal death, and rest in their graves, nothing can prevent their resurrection when Christ returns in power and glory; see Matthew 12:29; 16:18, 19; 18:18; 23:13; 28:18–20; Luke 11:52; John 20:23.

[19]*'Now write what you see,* namely the vision of the Son of Man, *what is,* that is, the current situation of these seven churches as seen from the point of view of the Lord in glory, *and what is to take place hereafter.'* Not so much a record of history from the first coming of Christ to the second coming, but a summing up of events of that age, including various aspects of the judgments of God, both those rescuing His own from the cruelties of this present evil world, and those punishing the unrighteous who side with God's enemies and their diabolic overlords.

[20]*'As for the mystery,* a mystery is a divinely revealed secret which could not be known otherwise than by divine revelation; *eg* the world could never have known the Son of God if the Father had not deigned to reveal Him, first prophetically in the Old Testament Scriptures, and then in the flesh of Jesus Christ, *of the seven stars which you saw in my right hand, and the seven golden lampstands, the seven stars are the angels of the seven churches,* Are they guardian angels? *cf* Michael, guardian archangel of Israel (Dan. 10:13, 21; Jude 9; Rev. 12:7); and the demonic guardian angel, of Persia (Dan. 10:13) and Greece (Dan. 10:20). Or do they represent the 'spirit' of the churches, that is, the prevailing

spiritual temperature? Or are they the human leaders, or overseers, or bishops, or chief elders—an angel being a messenger, whether angelic or human? Someone has put it like this: 'The stars which are the angels of the Churches are the churches as the Lord views them ideally in heaven as they shall be *and the seven lampstands are the seven churches.*' And the lampstands are the Churches as they actually are in their present state.

In view of the danger of a lampstand being taken away (*cf* 2:5), these must represent the light of God vouchsafed to churches which continue to deserve the light and glory and blessing of the Lord's presence in the local church.

Introduction
Chapters 2 and 3

The seven messages to seven churches are no mere literary device, like other elements in apocalyptic, but real messages, addressed to real, specific, historical churches. Some say they also represent successive periods in history; Ephesus the first century, Smyrna the period of persecution that followed, Pergamum the age of Constantine, Thyatira the Middle Ages, Sardis the Reformation era, Philadelphia the time of the modern missionary movement, and Laodicea the apostasy of the last days.

This would apply better to some ages than to others. For example, it is easier to fit the first and last ages into this scheme than some of the others. It is perhaps better, therefore, not to follow any strict sequence of interpretation, but to see the seven messages to the seven churches as covering the varied states or conditions of the whole church in all ages and in all places between the first and second comings of Christ. Thus, any of the seven messages can be applied to the church historically, in any day or in any place, locally or nationally.

The letters followed a general pattern, and the state of the various churches can be summarized thus: churches one and seven, Ephesus and Laodicea, are in grave danger; two and six, Smyrna and Philadelphia, 'in excellent shape' (Morris); three, four and five, Pergamum, Thyatira and Sardis, 'middling, neither very good, nor very bad.'

CHAPTER TWO

Letters to
Ephesus, Smyrna, Pergamum
and Thyatira
2:1–29

Ephesus (1–7)

Ephesus was the principal city of the province of Asia Minor, as Corinth was in Greece, and Rome in Italy. These three were the most important cities of that day, spread across the vast land-mass of the northern seaboard of the Mediterranean. Although Pergamum was the official capital of the province of Asia, Ephesus was the greatest city, not only of the province, but of all Asia Minor; the road from the East, from the River Euphrates indeed, ended there. It was a commercial and religious centre, with the great temple of Artemis, and every refined form of paganism including spiritism and the magical arts—very different from the grossness of Corinth. It was from Ephesus that 'all Asia heard the word of the Lord.' (Acts 19:10).

¹*'To the angel of the church in Ephesus write: "The words of him,* that is, the risen Christ, *who holds the seven stars in his right hand, who walks among the seven golden lampstands."* See Exodus 25:31–40. The 'seven' suggests the whole church in all ages held by Christ (Heb. 1:3b), who walks among them, which means that He is constantly in living touch with them to watch over them and provide the light of their witness to the world.

²*"I know your works, your toil and your patient endurance, and how you cannot bear evil men but have tested those who call themselves apostles,* The two biblical definitions of

29

apostles are: (1) those who had seen the risen Lord, see 1
Corinthians 25:5–9; (2) those who are in the foundation of
the church, see Ephesians 2:20, *but are not, and found them
to be false"'*; Paul in Acts 20:29 calls some in Ephesus
'grievous wolves', and there were such who travelled around
in peripatetic ministry (that is why there is so much about
hospitality in the New Testament) whose integrity had to be
tested, as *eg* in Corinth (2 Cor. 11:13–15).

    ³*"'I know you are enduring patiently and bearing up for my
name's sake, and you have not grown weary."'* This follows
from the presence of the invisible Christ walking up and
down among the churches. He knows all—the toil and
patience and, especially, the church's intolerance of evil
men arising both from their discernment to see, and their
courage to expose falsity. He also knows their patient forti-
tude amidst enemies; after all is he not (a very old man) a
prisoner in Patmos because of wicked persecution in
Ephesus, and the steadfastness which goes on being faithful
without tiring? He knows the whole situation as it deserves
commendation in His church, and He is not slow to give it.
(Compare also the apostle Paul's generous tributes to
churches and saints which deserve them.) Are we slow to
commend? It is not a Christian trait.

    ⁴*"'But I have this against you, that you have abandoned the
love you had at first."'* This is one of the saddest words in the
book and in the Bible, not only because of the fact stated, but
also because it happens to so many. It is not a matter of
losing the first emotional experience of conversion, for that
almost inevitable loss ought to lead to deeper faith, but it is
in turning away from the Lord Himself, because with carnal
zeal we become preoccupied with Christian service. The
danger cannot be exaggerated. It happens to many, who
then take refuge in formality; and it may happen to
preachers and Bible teachers who then become 'professional'!
Not even duteous devotions with 'quiet times', Bible readings
and devout religious observances will take the place of the
warm heart and tender love toward the Lord Jesus Himself.
This must be preserved at all costs. The Ephesians hated
what was wrong, but did not love the Lord as they had done.
This is curious, since hatred of wrong and love of the Lord

ought to go together; but in our minds we may piously profess the one to conceal the decline of the other. See Jeremiah 2:2, but from 2:1 to 3:5; also 2 Corinthians 11:2, 3.

⁵*"Remember, then, from what you have fallen, fallen from love, to hard labour; the former, a delight, the latter like a judicial sentence! repent and do the works you did at the first.* Perhaps the word 'repent' here is not so much a challenge to the sorrow which accompanies a change of heart, as the change itself from hard labour, with all the coldness, hardness and dryness associated with it, to service done in love of the Lord, and therefore for love of those served. *If not, I will come to you and remove your lampstand from its place, unless you repent."'* A church without love cannot remain a church. It may remain a group of Christians meeting together, but that is not the same. There are churches from whom the Lord has removed His lampstand. That is not to say that no Christian is present, but those remaining are in a state of backsliding, and the Spirit is so little wooed into the fellowship that the Lord has no pleasure from them and must necessarily withdraw His presence. It is fearful to know a fellowship of the Lord's people, formerly blessed, from whom the Lord has departed and it is 'Ichabod' with them—'the glory of the Lord has departed'. There are such, but, fortunately, God may be pleased to apprise them of their state so that at least one or two of their number may cry to God for mercy. In our day we have known such fellowships to be restored when God gave them another living, faithful pastor of the flock.

⁶*"Yet this you have, you hate the words of the Nicolaitans, which I also hate."'* No one really knows who the Nicolaitans were. The word means 'victorious people', and Irenaeus thinks the founder of the sect was the Nicholas of the deacons in Acts 6, but Clement of Alexandria says, 'No: if there was a rumour about Nicholas, he was really misunderstood.' We may associate the Nicolaitans here with Balaam mentioned in the letter to Pergamum, and possibly with Jezebel in the letter to Thyatira. These three churches all show the presence of groups or sects which were like a 'fifth column' within the church.

⁷*"He who has an ear, let him hear what the Spirit says to*

the churches. This challenge is given to each of the seven churches, or, rather, to individual Christians in them. *To him who conquers I will grant to eat of the tree of life, which is in the paradise of God."'* Seventeen times in the Revelation we have the words, 'To him who conquers': some have regarded the overcomers as a class of particularly heroic saints (*eg* G. H. Lang), but doubtless the reference is to all who in their earthly life by the victory of faith overcome satanic attempts to shake them out of that faith; see 1 John 5:4, 5.

The word 'paradise' is from the Persian 'park' and suggests the bliss of the presence of God. For the 'tree of life' and the 'tree of the knowledge of good and evil' see Genesis 3:4. Adam might eat of all the trees except the tree of the knowledge of good and evil, which meant that he might eat of the tree of life. He did not, and was later forbidden to do so, because he had first eaten of the tree of the knowledge of good and evil. If he had eaten of the tree of life after eating of the tree of knowledge of good and evil, he would presumably have become eternally sinful, a monstrosity only fit for hell! In fact, he would have become like the devil who had become his master and, possibly, as unsaveable as he.

Smyrna (8–11)

Smyrna was a great, planned and beautiful city at the head of its gulf. The Smyrnans worshipped the Emperor, and had erected a temple to Tiberius Caesar. The church is one of two in 'excellent shape' to whom the Spirit offers no criticism. Persecution saw to her refinement.

⁸*'And to the angel of the church in Smyrna write: "The words of the first and last,* compare 1:17, *who died and came to life."'*

⁹*'"I know your tribulation,* Polycarp, the great Christian who knew those who had seen Christ, including John, was martyred here in 155 AD. But there had been earlier persecutions: the Neronian Persecutions in which Paul had been martyred, and the Domitian Persecutions at the time, probably, John was writing (81–96 AD). Such Roman persecutions naturally had their repercussions in Roman

Smyrna. *and your poverty*, some suggest that the poverty was due to the plunder of hostile Jews. Remember what Paul suffered from Jews at various centres; (*but you are rich*). Wonderful contrast! *and the slander of those who say they are Jews and are not,* John is obviously reserving the word 'Jews' for those of Israelite descent who, as he would hold, ought naturally to have believed in Jesus Christ; compare Romans 2:28, 29 and Romans 9:6b; *but are a synagogue of Satan.*' Jesus in Matthew 23:33 called the scribes and Pharisees 'You serpents, you brood of vipers, how can you escape the damnation of hell?'

[10]'*"Do not fear what you are about to suffer.* How brave of the Spirit of God to speak so realistically to those about to suffer! It was better to fortify such than falsely console them, or conceal from them their coming trial. The value of such straight speaking is seen in the fact that some sixty or seventy years later Polycarp was brutally murdered for his steadfastness—a steadfastness he may very well have learned from these words. 'Fourscore and six years I have been his servant, and he hath done me no wrong. How then can I blaspheme my King who hath saved me?' So they burned him, but the flames, it is said, arched themselves round him and would not consume him, so they despatched him with a dagger! The Spirit of Christ, full of consolation, expects Christians to receive such awful knowledge as this courageously.

'*"Behold, the devil is about to throw some of you into prison, that you may be tested, and for ten days you will have tribulation."*' They were tested as Job was tested. Here the calamities which befall men of God are prophesied in terms of satanic attack. The Revelation is clear on this, which encourages those who in the second half of the twentieth 2nd Miller century are called to expose the deceptions of satanic powers — two in Christ's church preparatory to a new work of the Spirit. Part of this duty is to trace all sin back to Satan and lay it at his door, although not exonerating sinners from their part in sin's deeds. 'Ten days' suggests a limited testing, as in Job's case, for he was blessed (Job 42) in the end of his days.

'*"Be faithful unto death"*, Death is the logical end of such suffering, and since our Lord endured unto death without flinching and we are called to follow Him, we ought to be willing to do so even to that bitter end, if need be. Paul says of his sufferings for the sake of the church, that he is completing in his flesh (his share of) what is lacking in the afflictions of Christ, for the sake of His body, the church (Col. 1.24). *and I will give you the crown of life.*"' This is not the diadem, the royal crown, but the victory wreath (*stephanos*), which was appropriate for Stephen, the first Christian martyr. In Revelation 4:10 the living creatures cast their crowns (*stephanos*) before God.

¹¹'"*He who has an ear, let him hear what the Spirit says to the churches. He who conquers shall not be hurt by the second death.*"' See Revelation 20:6, 14; 21:8: the second death, or the lake of fire, is eternal death, or eternal punishment, the lot of those who enter mortal death without Christ. See also 1 Corinthians 15:54–57.

Pergamum (12–17)

Pergamum was the capital city of the province of Asia which became an independent kingdom after Alexander the Great: it was fifteen miles inland, had a wonderful library of two thousand parchment scrolls (the word 'Pergamum' comes from the word 'parchment'), and was a religious centre, particularly of Caesar worship. These facts are pertinent to the body of the letter. The church of Pergamum, Morris says, was 'middling'.

¹²'*And to the angel of the church in Pergamum write: "The words of him who has the sharp two-edged sword.*"' The reference to the sword may relate to the offiicial character of the city, with its Roman proconsul with power of life and death, see Romans 13:4. But there is a higher 'sword'. We think the two-edged sword may indicate the double judgment of God, on His own people, which is disciplinary, and on the unbelievers and the wicked, which is penal and final.

¹³'"*I know where you dwell, where Satan's throne is;* here, as we have noted before, sin is traced back to *its* author; *you hold fast my name and you did not deny my faith even in the days of Antipas*, we do not know who he was, *my witness.* The word 'witness' in the Greek is 'martyr', *my faithful one*,

a beautiful epithet for any one! *who was killed among you, where Satan dwells.*"' Evil is implacable, because its hatred of Christ and those who belong to him is absolute. What sort of evil was regnant in Pergamum to oppose the local church so directly? There were temples to Zeus, Dionysius and Athene in the city, as well as the temple dedicated to Augustus in 29 BC. This was subsequently followed by a second and third temple. Perhaps the reference to Satan's throne is, significantly, not to one centre of opposition to the gospel, but to many.

Some Christians have to live and work where the whole fabric of life is firmly opposed to godliness, and they marvel that people can be so adamantly hostile. The only adequate explanation is that Satan is enthroned there, and men in their various capacities are under his power.

[14]*'But I have a few things against you: you have some there who hold the teaching of Balaam, who taught Balak to put a stumbling block before the sons of Israel, that they might eat food sacrificed to idols and practice immorality.*"' The background to the Balaam story is found in Numbers chapters 22–25—with the clear implication from Numbers 31:16, 17 that Balaam, frustrated and bereft of his fee for cursing Israel, subtly seduced them by enticing their women to orgiastic and adulterous pagan worship. This led to a plague, and the slaughter of the guilty. Adultery and idolatry are always closely connected, whichever is prior. This is how Israel as a nation was ultimately ruined; see 1 Kings 11. Like king, like people! We see the danger much later in Paul's first Letter to the Corinthians, chapter 8.

[15]*"'So you also have some who hold the teaching of the Nicolaitans.*"' It is clearly by this teaching that Satan's throne is present, not only in the sense of the general satanic rule of the city over against the Christian church, but also in that Satan was secretly instilling some of his poison into the church itself. It takes superior discernment and constant resolution to resist the enveloping influences of paganism.

[16]*"'Repent then. If not, I will come to you soon and war against them with the sword of my mouth.*"' If the Lord's soldiers do not maintain an attitude of war towards the evils among which they dwell, the Lord will come and war against

them for neglecting His war. This war can be waged only by the sword of the Spirit which is the Word of God (Eph 6:17). It is therefore amazing that Christian leaders at home and abroad lament the state of the local and national Church when the truth is that the Word has not been thoroughly applied to their situation. Where the Word has been so applied and its fruits are manifest, the charge may be levelled by critical Christian leaders that such faithful ministry is too upsetting. But it is the price of Christian advance. The choice is clear, but the tortuous carnal mind seeks other more placatory ways. There is none.

[17]*"He who has an ear, let him hear what the Spirit says to the churches. To him who conquers I will give some of the hidden manna,* The word 'manna' means, 'What is it?' or, 'It is a gift, or portion', see Exodus 16:32–34. Israel did not know what it was, but they knew it was heavenly bread, see Deuteronomy 8:3, and also Hebrews 9:4. There is a Jewish legend that before the destruction of Jerusalem by the Chaldeans, the ark and its contents were hidden by Jeremiah at Sinai in the hope that they would be manifested in the days of Messiah. There is no evidence that Jeremiah believed such a thing, but the hidden manna is undoubtedly the secret bread of the Word of God which sustains afflicted servants of God in their day of trouble until their enemies marvel at their steadfastness and strength; see Matthew 4:11. *and I will give him a white stone with a new name written on the stone which no one knows except him who receives it."'* There are at least seven ideas as to the origin and meaning of the white stone: (1) it was used for a vote by a juror; (2) it was a counter for reckoning; (3) a superstitious symbol of a happy, or 'red-letter' day; (4) it was a 'ticket' to food or entertainment; (5) an amulet for good luck; (6) it represented manna which fell from heaven with precious stones (see Morris, p.68); (7) it was a stone on the high priest's breastplate with the name of the tribe written on it, see the reference to Urim in Exodus 28:30. In spiritual terms, surely it means that each individual Christian may have a secret with the Lord that none other can share; the importance of that being that the individual believer may enjoy a relationship with the Lord which is unique and

which therefore sets an inestimable value upon each soul in God's sight.

Thyatira (18–29)

'Thyatira,' says Sir William Ramsay, 'was the least important city in the area, but it had many trade guilds.' (Morris, p.69). Lydia, the seller of purple (Acts 16:14), came from Thyatira. It was famous for wool dyeing. Morris says the church was 'middling'; but it is remarkable that although Thyatira was in some ways the least important city, it was very busy industrially, and if there were deep tensions in the church, it was, nevertheless, lively. Indeed, it evoked from the Spirit the longest letter of the seven!

[18]'*And to the angel of the church in Thyatira write: "The words of the Son of God, who has eyes like a flame of fire*, see 1:14, *and whose feet are like burnished* if not burning, *bronze."'* See 1:15.

[19]'*"I know your words, your love and faith and service, and patient endurance, and that your latter works exceed the first."'* This church under trial was improving, whereas the Ephesian church was growing cold (2:4).

[20]'*"But I have this against you, that you tolerate the woman Jezebel,* some manuscripts read 'thy woman', suggesting that the leader of the fellowship was in some association with a particularly unworthy woman: we do not know; *who calls herself a prophetess and is teaching and beguiling my servants to practise immorality and to eat food sacrificed to idols."* This subject goes back to Balaam (see Revelation 2:14 and Numbers chs. 22—25 and 31). Paul also deals with it in two letters: 1 Corinthians 6:14–18; and chapters 8—9; and Romans chapters 14—15. To inveigle the people of God into Pagan worship, in order to destroy them, was Satan's chief strategy. It began generally by inviting the people of God to mix extraneous worship with their own. Mixed worship (syncretism) was the danger of the high places. Mixed marriages also led to this; see 1 Kings 11. The worship of the calves at Bethel and Dan, after the division of the kingdoms, was of this nature, and when the pagans from the east replaced the ten tribes of Israel, the people, thereafter called

Samaritans, mixed their worship; see 2 Kings 17.

The same problem arose in Corinth and, apparently, in Rome. The question for Christians was: how far were they to associate with pagans in a preponderantly heathen environment? The principle, surely, is that Christians mix with unbelieving people for *their* good as far as they are able to keep themselves pure from sinful contamination. This is largely a matter of the individual conscience before God, although guidance and counsel may often be sought and given.

[21]"*I gave her time,* note God's patience! *to repent, but she refuses to repent of her immorality.* [22]*Behold, I will throw her on a sick bed,* which is different, as Dean Farrar observes, from a bed of love, see 1 Corinthians 11:29, 30, *and those who commit adultery with her I will throw into great tribulation, unless they repent of her doings*; note the attempt to separate her from those associated with her in sinning; [23]*and I will strike her children dead.* This is a fearful statement. Does it refer to natural, or spiritual children— the latter, followers? It is painful to see parents who have turned aside from God or who have persecuted his servants, eventually suffering broken hearts on account of their children's misdeeds. Was this a reference to pestilence or plague? *And all the churches shall know that I am he who searches mind and heart,* see Jeremiah 11:20; Hebrews 4:11–13; *and I will give to each of you as your works deserve.*" See 2 Corinthians 5:10; Revelation 20:12; 22:12; also the necessity of 'works of faith' as proof of the reality, in James 2:22, 26.

[24]"*But to the rest of you in Thyatira, who do not hold this teaching, who have not learned what some call the deep things of Satan*, Who calls them the deep things of Satan? Were these satanists so bold? Or did they profess the deep things to be of God? See 1 Corinthians 2:9, 19; 2 Corinthians 2:11; *to you I say, I do not lay upon you any other burden*; for if you have resisted that, you have done well! [25]*only hold fast what you have, until I,* Christ, *come.*" Advance in the Christian life is not always gained by seeming advance. Standing one's ground, against pressure or force, is action, and calls for expenditure of energy. Our Lord's words in

John 15:4, 'Abide in me', and in 1 John 2:24, 27, 28 and Paul's word 'stand' in Ephesians 6:11, 13, 14, are all active: compare Moses at Rephidim (Exod. 17:8–13); Job also, and Jesus on the cross. Long-suffering, patient endurance and the like, all call for active resistance.

[26]'"*He who conquers and who keeps my works until the end, I will give him power (authority, exousia* not *dunamis) over the nations,* see 1 Corinthians 6:2, and Psalm 2, [27]*and he shall rule them,* that is, he shall shepherd them, see Matthew 28:18–20, *with a rod of iron,* the rod is for firmness, *as when earthen pots are broken in pieces, even as I myself have received power,* the word 'power' is not in the Greek: does it imply *exousia* (authority), verse 26? *from my Father;* [28]*and I will give him the morning star.*"' 'The bright and morning star' (22:16). The angels, probably the first in creation, are called 'morning stars' in Job 38:7. Perhaps 'morning' suggests prime authority, and 'star', glory.

[29]'"*He who has an ear, let him hear what the Spirit says to the churches.*"'

CHAPTER THREE

Letters to Sardis, Philadelphia and Laodicea
3:1-22

Sardis (1-6)

Five roads led to and from Sardis, a commercial and wealthy city commanding the Hermus valley. The people of Sardis fondly imagined their city set on a precipitous hill-top was impregnable, but twice it was conquered, by Cyrus in 549 BC, and by Antiochus III in 218 BC. It was a centre for the worship of Cybele. An earthquake took place there in AD 17. She is another of the 'middling' churches, although there is no word of heresy or vile practice in her.

¹'*And to the angel of the church in Sardis write "The words of him who has the seven spirits of God,* compare 1:4 *and the seven stars."'* These are the angels of the seven churches (1:20).

'"*I know your works;* compare 2:26; *you have the name of being alive*, much activity, always something new, *and you are dead.* Paul says the very opposite of the faithful: 'as dying, and behold we live; as punished, and yet not killed.' (2 Cor: 6:9) ²*Awake, and strengthen what remains and is on the point of death, for I have not found your works perfect* not completed *in the sight of my God."'* The exalted Christ knows where each church stands as to its spiritual state as to the relative maturity and immaturity (see 1 Corinthians 3:1-3a; Hebrews 5:12; 6:1a). The works of the Sardis church seem not to have been works of mercy and love, but self-regarding.

³*'Remember then what you received and heard; keep that,* which implies that they had departed from it, *and repent.* Such recovery requires us to reconsider what is already given, and therefore look for new treasure in the old; see Matthew 13:52. It is a work of the Spirit of God to awaken somnolent souls and quicken complacent minds and hearts to see the old Scriptures in new light. To the sensitive spirit it is a marvel that God constantly does this. *If you will not awake, I will come like a thief,* that is, suddenly—and *any* coming is a surprise to those who are asleep—*and you will not know at what hour I will come upon you.'"* This suggests a coming for disciplinary judgment rather than the Second Coming.

⁴*'"Yet you have still a few names* in the church *in Sardis people who have not soiled their garments*; with the soiling of unfaithfulness: even these few are described in negative terms, yet doubtless they preserved the church in Sardis from complete deadness, like the few who through Abraham's intercession would have saved Sodom and Gomorrah from destruction if their number had been sufficient (Gen 18:16–33); *and they shall walk with me in white, for they are worthy.'"* (Ps. 104:2a) The question arises whether references to white garments in the Revelation 3:5, 18; 4:4; 6:11; 7:9, 13, 14; 19:8, 14) speak more of justification (the standing of the saints) than of sanctification (their state). Probably in most, if not all instances, both. Certainly, works of faith as evidence of Christian character are, according to James 2:18–26, the sine qua non of reward hereafter; see 1 Corinthians 3:15, but see under.

⁵*'"He who conquers shall be clad thus in white garments, and I will not blot his name out of the book of life;* The negative and seemingly non-predestinarian concept of blotting out could come from Moses (Exod. 32:32) and Paul (Rom. 9:3). We may think of the Lord's covenanted people, as eg in Genesis chapter 17, as under probation during their earthly life; compare John 6:66. Since the white robe is associated with not being blotted out of the book of life, it would appear that here it represents primarily basic salvation, or justification. *I will confess his name before my Father and before his angels.'"* See Matthew 10:32, 33.

[6]*"'He who has an ear, let him hear what the Spirit says to the churches.'"*

Philadelphia (7–13)

Philadelphia was set at a junction of three roads leading to the provinces of Mysia, Lydia and Phrygia. It was a gateway to the east, and a centre for the expansion of Greek culture and influence. The city was set in an area of hot springs, where a very serious earthquake had taken place in AD 70, affecting both Philadelphia itself and other surrounding cities. The Philadelphians worshipped Dionysius, the son of Zeus. The chief feature of the church was that she had no enemies within her fellowship, but without. She, with Smyrna, is given an excellent report, with no adverse criticism.

[7]*"And to the angel of the church in Philadelphia write: "The words of the holy one, the true one, who has the key of David, who opens and no one shall shut, who shuts and no one opens."'* This quotation, taken from Isaiah 22:22, represents the city of David as the heavenly Jerusalem and the kingdom of Christ, and indicates the authority vested in Messiah to open and shut, that is, to include or exclude according to His gracious will: 'I have the keys of Death and Hades.' (Rev. 1:18). See also Matthew 16:18, 19; 28:18–20 and Revelation 5:5 for Christ's power over death, redemptively won to employ the key to deliver His own from the realms of death and to bequeath to His servants His authority through the gospel to preserve believing souls from the dominion of mortal death and from the penalty of the second or eternal death; see Revelation 20:6, 14; 21:8. 'No one comes to the Father, but by me.' (John 14:6) 'He only could unlock the gate of heaven, and let us in.' (C. F. Alexander, 'There is a green hill far away').

[8]*"'I know your works. Behold, I have set before you an open door, which no one is able to shut;* this means that God had provided wonderful openings for the Philadelphian Christians to preach the gospel, including the gift of utterance (Acts 2:4; 1 Cor. 1:5; 2 Cor. 8:7; Eph. 6:19). This is the first reference in these letters to evangelistic outreach

because preservation must come first, but continuing life requires outlet, implying also willing ears and hearts to respond, see 2 Corinthians 2:12; Colossians 4:3; Acts 14:27. *I know that you have but little power*, better 'I know that you have a little power': there is no suggestion of disparagement of their power (dynamic) in the original; *and yet you have kept my word and have not denied my name."'* There is no call for 'yet'; the tone of the original is wholly commendatory. This sentence, 'I know you have a little power and you have kept my word and not denied my name,' can be understood only as building up to the following climax, not detracting from it. The suggestion seems to be that keeping the Lord's Word and not denying His name are more determinative of spiritual success in evangelical outreach than the degree of spiritual power the church may be seen to have at any moment. Faithfulness is bound ultimately to be rewarded with fruitfulness, for faithfulness shakes enemies, since they can do nothing against it. The Lord of glory was slain because He could not be moved.

The result is: ⁹*"'Behold, I will make those of the synagogue of Satan who say that they are Jews and are not, but lie*—see Revelation 2:9; Romans 2:28, 29; 9:6, 7; *behold, I will make them come and bow down before your feet, and learn that I have loved you."'* Does this mean that these wicked Jews will be converted? It seems so; for this result of faithfulness seems to point to the conversion of hostile Jews throughout the entire dispensation, where Christian faithfulness to Jesus and the consequent open door of God's opportunity cause enmity to be broken down (see Eph. 2:13–15) and Jews to be brought into the faith. And this points forward to the great enlightening of the Jews when they will see their Messiah, whom they pierced, coming in power and glory, see Zechariah 12:10; John 19:34; Revelation 1:7; and Romans 11:12–15.

¹⁰*"'Because you have kept my word of patient endurance, I will keep you from the hour of trial which is coming on the whole world, to try those who dwell upon the earth."'* The words *'keep you from' (ek=out of)* could mean 'save them from it' or 'keep them in it'. If the former, 'save them from it', a doctrine of the rapture of the church cannot be constructed

upon so slender a point. Besides, the messages to the seven churches indicate the several states and conditions of the universal church during the span of time between the comings of Christ. Whether the promise is to keep saints in the midst of particular trial, or to enable them to escape it, in either case the blessed protection is a reward for faithfulness, and doubtless the promise is given as an incentive to the church to be faithful everywhere, and at all times (2:10).

[11]'"*I am coming soon*; could mean in interim or final judgment, for a profound sense of the Lord's power gives a sense of imminence to His coming; *hold fast what you have, so that no one may seize your crown.* The crown (*stephanos*) is the victory wreath or garland awarded for personal faithfulness. It is first, the 'crown of life' (Jas. 1:12; Rev. 2:10), or the 'crown of righteousness' (2 Tim. 4:8), then the 'unfading crown of glory' (1 Pet. 5;4). [12]*He who conquers*, by resisting the diabolical intention of all trial and testing and therefore holding fast, *I will make him a pillar in the temple of my God*; see Ephesians 2:21. God will dwell in a house of living stones. Paul portrays the church as a building of which Jesus Christ is the only foundation (1 Cor. 3:11), but in which the Apostles and New Testament prophets are next in the foundation, then the rest including living stones and pillars built right up to the Top Stone, Christ; see Ephesians 2:20, 21; 1 Peter 2:4–7: also Jeremiah 1:18; Galatians 2:9; 1 Timothy 3:15. *never shall he go out of it*, pillars should not move! (Pss. 23:6b; 27:4), *and I will write on him the name of my God,* He will be named by the name of the Father, says the Spirit, *and the name of the city of my God, the new Jerusalem which comes down from my God out of heaven*, that is, the name of Christ's church, which, of course, bears His name, *and my own new name.*"' This most naturally refers to the Holy Spirit, who, as the next verse shows, is writing to the churches. (It is interesting to recall that the city of Philadelphia had had two other *names* Neocaesarea, and Flavia: the Philadelphians would appreciate the point.)

[13]'"*He who has an ear, let him hear what the Spirit says to the churches.*"'"

Laodicea (14–22)

Laodicea was set at the junction of the Lycus and Maeander valleys, at the intersection of three roads commanding the approaches to Phrygia. It was one of the richest commercial centres in the world, famous for its black wool, its medical school, its banking system, and its seat of judiciary. There was a colony of Jews in the city comprising 7,000 adult males, who were allowed their own laws. There was a letter of Paul to the Laodiceans (Col. 4:15, 16), which is either lost, or is identical with the (circular) letter to the Ephesians (the word 'Ephesians' is not found in the many manuscripts of Ephesians 1:1).

[14]'And to the angel of the church in Laodicea write: "The words of the Amen, the faithful and true witness, see the 'God of truth', in Isaiah 65:16, *the beginning of God's creation.*"' The 'beginning' cannot mean that Christ, the 'Amen' and 'faithful and true witness' is Himself the first part of creation, although Paul also calls Him the 'first-born' of (or over) all creation' (Col. 1:15). He belongs to the uncreated Godhead (John 1:1–3, 9–13). Barclay calls Him the 'moving cause', and Caird the 'source', but perhaps 'beginning' here should be rendered 'beginner'; see also Hebrews 1:1–3.

[15]'*I know your works; you are neither cold nor hot. Would that you were cold or hot!* The Spirit speaks as if God were in a dilemma, without evidence upon which to assess this church. But such lack of ability to assess is only apparent, for God is displeased with those who eqivocate and naughtily seek to suspend necessary judgment. He would rather be done with them; see 2 Peter 2:21.

[16]*So, because you are lukewarm, and neither cold nor hot, I will spew you out of my mouth.* One reading renders 'I am likely to spew you.' But we must not weaken the force of the words, for that would insist on a neutrality where God permits none. Neither, 'He who is not with me is against me,' (Matt. 12:30; Luke 11:23) nor, 'he that is not against us is for us,' (Mark 9:40; Luke 9:50) allows neutrality. [17]*For you say, I am rich, I have prospered, and I need nothing*; contrast Smyrna, 2:9; *not knowing that you are wretched, pitiable,*

poor, in a wealthy commercial city! *blind*, where a medical school would have easy access to the famous Phrygian eye-salve, *and naked."'* Laodicea was a centre for wool and clothing!

[18]*"'Therefore I counsel you to buy from me* (Is 55:1–3) *gold refined by fire*, see Job 23:10; 1 Pet. 1:7, *that you may be rich*, The contrast is between material and spiritual wealth. Like the man in our Lord's parable (Luke 12:16–21) who prided himself on his wealth of goods, had everything money could buy, but not the spiritual coinage of faith, nor the sense of need, which the 'poor in spirit' is aware of, to make him 'hunger and thirst for righteousness'; they were bereft of spiritual blessings. *and white garments*, see the robe of Christ's righteousness (Is. 61:10; Rom. 10:3; 2 Cor 5:21b; Phil. 3:9), *to clothe you and to keep the shame of your nakedness from being seen*, see Genesis 3:21; 2 Corinthians 5:1–5; Colossians 3:9, 10, 12–14, *and salve to anoint your eyes, that you may see*. The salve is God's Word: 'The unfolding of thy words gives light; it imparts understanding to the simple.' (Ps 119:130). [19]*Those whom I love, I reprove and chasten; so be zealous and repent."'* See Proverbs 3:21; 1 Corinthians 11:32; Hebrews 12:7–11.

[20]*"'Behold I stand at the door and knock; if any one hears my voice and opens the door*, behold Christ's amazing respect for the will of the individual, as if to say, 'Is there one Christian in Laodicea who will invite me into his heart?' 'If so, says Christ by the Spirit, *I will come in to him and eat with him, and he with me*. This is an invitation to the full, family life with the Lord, a domestic privilege which enables the soul receiving the Lord not only to enjoy Him, but to conquer all satanic attempts to quench his love for Him (2:4), or cool his ardour (3:15, 16). *¹He who conquers, I will grant him to sit with me on my throne, see Matthew 19:28; 1 Corinthians 6:2, 3; Revelation 20:4, 6b; 22:5b, as I myself conquered,* by His victorious death, see eg Philippians 2:5–11; Colossians 2:15; Hebrews 1:1–4; 2:9–14, *and sat down with my father on his throne."'* The sublimity of this promise beginning with the simple domesticity of His coming to eat in our home is beyond all imagination.

[29]*"'He who has an ear, let him hear what the Spirit say to*

the churches."' William Hendriksen states, 'These seven churches represent the entire Church during the entire dispensation.' (*More than Conquerors*, p.97). We have, then, a conspectus of the state of the churches in all ages in all places, along with what the Spirit is saying to them in their various states and circumstances. It is ours to apply the message or messages to our own situation. It may be added, that a study of the promises to overcomers in the seven churches will prove thought-provoking and fruitful.

CHAPTER FOUR

The Glory of the
Almighty Creator
4:1–11

We now plunge into the mysteries of the book of the
Revelation, and into its second division (chapters 4—7),
which takes us again from the first to the second coming of
Christ.

A thought, which may be helpful hereafter, is that John
who was 'in the Spirit on the Lord's day', may have spent
much time on Patmos reading the (Old Testament)
Scriptures, which, of course, would have been ground upon
which the Spirit could cause to flourish the wonderful
visions and truths about to be unfolded. Basil Atkinson, late
of Cambridge University library, said that there is hardly a
'wisp' of words in Revelation which cannot be traced to some
reference in the Old Testament.

Chapters 4 and 5 stand by themselves somewhat apart
from chapter 6 and 7, affording visions of God the Creator
(chapter 4) and God the Redeemer Judge, Jesus Christ
Himself (chapter 5).

¹*After this I looked, and lo, in heaven*, not the heavenly
places where created spirit beings are in conflict (Job 1; Dan.
10; Eph. 6:10–18), but, suggests Hendriksen, the whole
universe (during the time between the comings) viewed
from the aspect of God's throne; *an open door!* see Ezekiel
1:1; Matthew 3:16; Acts 7:54–60: the 'open door' indicates the
clarity of vision accorded to John. *And the first voice, which I
had heard speaking to me like a trumpet, said, 'Come up
hither, and I will show you what must take place after this.'*

We are advised not to take 'after this' in the programmatic or dispensational sense, since this is a new experience of the Spirit, as the words which follow show.

[2]At once I was in the Spirit, This was a unique experience accorded to John and one which puts the Apostles in a class by themselves, both as to their being set in the foundations of the church (Eph 2:20) and as communicators of the full and final Word of God, to which nothing may be added (Rev. 22:18, 19). *and lo, a throne stood in heaven, with one seated on the throne!* John's inability to describe the one on the throne indicates the impenetrable nature of the essential glory of God.

[3]And he who sat there appeared, Ezekiel 1:26 dares to express this in terms of a human form, but John does not do so. One of the best descriptions of the indescribable glory of the unseen and eternal God is that He is 'in light inaccessible hid from our eyes' so that it is 'only the splendour of light hideth Thee.' (Walter Chalmers Smith, 'Immortal, Invisible, God Only Wise') *like jasper and carnelian*, these probably representing respectively, the diamond (Rev. 21:11) and the ruby (the first and last stones on the high priest's breastplate, see Exod. 28:17–20). White and red present the biblical mind with no difficulties in the interpretation of their symbolism! White certainly stands for the holiness and purity of God, while red may represent redemption, but perhaps even more probably, the judgments of God. *and round the throne was a rainbow that looked like an emerald.* This goes beyond all natural science and human understanding. J. B. Phillips calls it 'a halo like an emerald rainbow', which may be regarded as representing the mercy of God, but the word for 'emerald' has 'crashing' associations which may suggest a prism affording all colours of the rainbow.

[4]Round the throne were twenty-four thrones, and seated on the thrones were twenty-four elders, Who are the elders? The number is surely suggestive of the twelve tribes of Israel and the twelve apostles of the Lamb, representing the Old and New Testament saints together (see Rev. 21:12–14; but see also 1 Chron. 24:7–19; 25:9–30): or, as Hendriksen says, 'the entire church' Charles says, 'They are angels

50 *A Vision of Glory*

representing the faithful': Morris thinks they are probably
angels, quoting Isaiah 24:23; but E. J. Young assumes they
are elders of the Church. Certainly the redeemed are, of all
creatures, next to God, see Genesis 1:26, 27; Hebrews 2:6–8.
clad in white garments, with golden crowns (wreaths) *upon
their heads.* It is suggested that saints would not wear
crowns before the Lamb assumed authority, but surely this
is too programmatic.

⁵*From the throne issue flashes of lightning, and voices and
peals of thunder,* cf Exodus 19:16–19; 20:18–20, *and before
the throne burn seven torches of fire, which are the seven
spirits of God*; see also 1:4; 3:1; 5:6. These represent the
sevenfold, that is, the completely comprehensive operations
of the Holy Spirit; ⁶*and before the throne there is as it were a
sea of glass, like crystal.* The crystal sea speaks of the
absolute transparency of the divine character and His
works in purity and righteousness, whereas the fact of the
sea probably suggests the unapproachableness of the
Almighty, 'who alone has immortality and dwells in unapproachable light, whom no man has ever seen or can see.
To him be honour and eternal dominion. Amen.' (1 Tim.
6:16) Although by grace we become children of God, we are
adopted children (Rom. 8:15; Gal. 4:5), and never partake of
the Godhead: our Lord always preserves the distinction
between His unique relationship with the Father and ours,
and never says 'our Father, although He bids us say it.

*And round the throne, on each side of the throne, are four
living creatures, full of eyes in front and behind*: The twenty-
four elders are described before the living creatures, which
latter are surely cherubim (see Ezek. 1:4–14; 10:20–22),
because the saints are higher in rank than all angelic beings
(see Gen. 1:26, 27; 1 Cor. 6:3; Heb. 1:14; 2:5, 16). ⁷*the first
living creature like a lion, the second living creature like an
ox, the third living creature with the face of a man, and the
fourth living creature like a flying eagle.* See Ezekiel 1:10
and 10:14; but the order is different here. To the rabbis the
four symbols suggested the finest elements in nature,
including man, although in Ezekiel 1:10; 10:14 and here,
they are attributed to angelic beings (see above on v.6). It
was Irenaeus who first identified the four symbols with the

four evangelists representing the four portraits of the one Jesus Christ in the Gospels; but Irenaeus, Victorinus, and Augustine all pinned the four symbols differently to the four Gospels. As far as such identification is helpful, the order probably best fitting the four Gospels portraits of Christ is: the lion—Christ as King of the Jews, in Matthew; the ox—Jesus the obedient Servant, in Mark; the man—Jesus in His humanity, in Luke; the eagle—Jesus Christ as the eternal Son, in John.

[8]*And the four living creatures, each of them with six wings,* Ezekiel 1:6, four wings; Isaiah 6:2, seraphim, six wings, *are full of eyes all round and within, and day and night,* no night there, but 'day and night' express constancy in our terms, *they never cease to sing, 'Holy, holy, holy, is the Lord God Almighty, who was and is and is to come!'* Remember that the world 'holy' means 'apart' or 'separate'. The three tenses of the Lord God Almighty's existence express eternity. [9]*And whenever,* temporal suggestion again, *the living creatures give glory and honour and thanks to him who is seated on the throne, who lives for ever and ever.* [10]*the twenty-four elders fall down before him who is seated on the throne and worship him who lives for ever and ever; they cast their crowns before the throne, singing,* [11]*'Worthy art thou, our Lord and God, to receive glory and honour and power, for thou didst create all things, and by thy will they existed and were created.'*

From this climax of the chapter it is good to look back through it and see how the elements of the vision add up to the theme of the word-picture of the Creatorhood of God. All is created by Him, and for Him (Rom. 11:36; col. 1:16; Heb. 1:2; 11:3). The God who created all things for Himself and for His purposes is altogether transcendant. See the frequent references to the unique Otherness of the Lord in Is. 41:4, 26–28; 42:8; 43:10–13; 44:6–8, 24; 45:5, 6, 14, 18, 21, 22; 46:9; 47:8, 10; 48:12.

God is other than His creatures and is guarded from intrusion by the awesome spiritual phenomena which surround His throne. He is also guarded by archangels who by their character understand the purpose beyond creation, which is redemption; and they utter perpetually before His throne the three-fold, 'Holy, holy, holy,' which in prosaic language means, 'Separate' or 'Other', the Lord God Almighty, the Eternal. These, as God's servants and the servants of the redeemed (Heb. 1:14), prompt the saints to cast their crowns before Him and sing the song of the Creator. This is the attitude which saints on earth must cultivate constantly, lest they become preoccupied with such thoughts of secondary causes as may lead them to detract from the glory and the power of the Almighty, and His right to do as He wills with His own, and to do it well. Alexander Solzhenitzyn says, 'Men who believe only in themselves fall victims to their captors and are destroyed.' The psalmist David said, 'Lead me to the Rock which is higher than I.' Shall not the Creator, and therefore the Judge of all the earth do right?

James Philip in *The New Bible Dictionary* says that 'God created the world "for the manifestation of the glory of His eternal power, wisdom and goodness" (*Westminster Confession*). Creation, in other words, is theocentric, and intended to display the glory of God; to be, as Calvin says, "the theatre of His glory".' (p. 270).

CHAPTER FIVE

The Redeemer
5:1–14

The vision continues: *¹And I saw in the right hand of him who was seated on the throne a scroll written within and on the back, sealed*, perfectly, *with seven seals*; The scroll contains the divine Creator's will concerning the world's destiny, especially as to judgment. Indeed, the Revelation is a book of the judgment of God in the widest sense, describing prophetically the vindication and triumph of the Almighty in history, see Acts 17;31. *²and I saw a strong angel proclaiming with a loud voice,* the matter is momentous, *'Who is worthy to open the scroll and break its seals?'* that is, to open the scroll and progressively break the seals in seven stages (6.1).

³And no one in heaven or on earth or under the earth, the three locations comprising 'everywhere' (see Exod. 20:4; Phil. 2:10): 'the third division has become synonymous with Hades.' (Charles) *was able to open the scroll or to look into it*, Obviously much more than merely opening and looking into the scroll is implied here: it is the ability to cope with the total world situation, including creation, redemption and judgment, which gives the right to open the scroll. *⁴and I, John, wept much that no one was found worthy to open the scroll or look into it.* We are conscious here of the sensitivity of the apostle John, accentuated to the highest degree by an elevation of spirit to feel the keenest distress that no one in the whole creation was found able to open the

53

scroll, as if the Almighty was hindered in His purposes of creation and redemption.

⁵*Then one of the elders said to me, 'Weep not; lo, the Lion of the tribe of Judah, the Root of David, has conquered, so that he can open the scroll and its seven seals.'* That an 'elder' informs John, inclines us to the view that these elders are saints, for this is not the province or preserve of angels, nor do they know or understand the judgments of God involved in redemption. As to the 'Lion of the tribe of Judah', see Genesis 49:9; Ezekiel 19:2, 3, 5, 6; also 2 Esdras 12:31. For the 'Root of David', see Isaiah 53:2; also Revelation 22:16; but see Isaiah 11:1, 10 for 'shoot' not 'Root': 'conquered' refers to Christ's victorious death and resurrection, see Hebrews 5:7–9. Verse 6 should not be separated from verse 5. The Lion and the Lamb are one.

⁶*And between the throne and the four living creatures and among the elders, I saw a Lamb,* compare the Lion and the Lamb: the setting of the Lamb suggests His overall dominance of the scene; *standing, as though it had been slain*; speaking of the eternality of sacrificial love the earthly, redeeming experience of our risen Lord being beautifully recorded, there are 27 references to the Lamb after this, see particularly v.12; 7:14, 17; 12:11; 13:8; 14:10; 15:3; 17:12–14; 19:7, 8; 21:22. *with seven horns and with seven eyes, which are the seven spirits of God sent out into all the earth*; the authority Christ gained by His redeeming work is now at the universal disposal of the Spirit of God, following our Lord's enthronement as King and His installation as Judge, see John 16:7–11; ⁷*and he went and took the scroll from the right hand of him who was seated on the throne.*

⁸*And when he had taken the scroll, the four living creatures and the twenty-four elders fell down before the Lamb, each* elder *holding a harp,* for praise, *and with golden bowls full of incense, which are the prayers of the saints*; The incense symbolises the prayers of the saints (Ps. 141:2); and it is clear from the context, especially the song about to be recorded, that these are prayers of praise of the worthiness of the Lamb to take the book and open the seals, since he has conquered by His death and resurrection. ⁹*and they sang a*

new song, saying, The word 'new' emphasises that the divine events pictorialised in John's vision are newly revealed in the sense that without this key revelation, none could understand the meaning of the universe and the Almighty's purposes in it and for it.

'*Worthy art thou to take the scroll and to open its seals, for thou wast slain and by thy blood didst ransom men for God from every tribe and tongue and people and nation,* the members of this list are taken from Daniel 3, [10]*and hast made them,* the ambiguity of the 'them' is explained by the fact that the song is sung by the living (angelic) creatures and the elders, *a kingdom,* not 'kings' as in AV, *and priests to our God,* all believers are priests (see 1 Pet. 2:5, 9) offering up spiritual sacrifices to God in the one, only and all-acceptable sacrifice of Christ, *and they shall reign on,* rather, over, *earth.*' The kingdom of priests is gained by the obedience and merit of the Redeemer's sacrifice. He is, therefore, worthy to take the scroll and open the seals to reveal God's dealings with the universe of men and things on the ground of the Lion/Lamb's appearance in history. This He does by declaring in word and deed the standard of divine judgment—and by finally rectifying all things, in, through, and for Christ. That this is no partial or partisan opinion, John proves by saying:

[11]*Then I looked, and I heard around the throne and the living creatures and the elders the voice of many angels, numbering myriads of myriads and thousands of thousands* (Dan. 7:10b), [12]*saying with a loud voice,* this is the chorus presumably of all the angelic throng, who sum up this magnificat in a burst and build-up of cumulative praise, '*Worthy is the Lamb,* why not the Lion? because the contrast is between the right of the Redeemer as Judge to reveal and execute the vindicating and God-glorifying judgments upon all things, and the humiliating cost of redemption as the Man of Sorrows, acquainted with grief, and despised and rejected by men (Isa. 53); *who was slain, to receive power* (1 Cor. 1:24) *and wealth* (2 Cor. 8:9; Eph. 3:8) *and wisdom* (1 Cor. 1:24) *and might* (Eph. 6:10; 2 Thess. 1:9) *and honour* (Heb. 2:9; Phil. 2:11) *and glory* (John 1:14; Heb. 2:9) *and blessing!*' (Mark 11:9)

There are seven ascriptions here, a fitting number, summing up not only all that the eternal Son from all eternity has been in His divine Sonship, and all that He was as the perfect God/Man, but also all that accrues to Him for the perfections, infinite costs, and supreme triumphs of His redeeming work. This is an 'all stops out' chorus, in which even angelic and redeemed human strength are taxed to the utmost to express with worthy fulness the unsurpassable and inexpressible excellencies of the Saviour. But it is only then that the full glory of the acclamation is heard, when John says: [13]*And I heard every creature in heaven and on earth and under the earth and in the sea, and all therein,* that is to say, the whole creation (which must include the damned, Phil. 2:10, 11) at the climactic, consummating and eternal moment of judgment conspiring to focus the attention of all things in heaven, and on earth, and under it, upon the Lamb: there is no opposition to this, no other voice, no other thought in any creature's mind but, Glory to the Lamb! *saying, 'To him who sits upon the throne and to the Lamb,* they are eternally One, *be blessing and honour and glory and might for ever and ever!'* The last four of the former seven attributes are repeated in different order. Does this not suggest the infinite variations of the theme of praise which are possible to worshipping creatures?

[14]*And the four living creatures said, 'Amen!' and the elders fell down and worshipped.* The instant response of the living creatures and the devout action of the elders approve the united praise of all creation, and complete the doxology.

CHAPTER SIX

The Seals
6:1–17

In this second section of the Revelation (chapters 4—7), which covers the span between the two comings of Christ, we have seen thus far the visions of God the Creator in chapter 4, and God the Redeemer in chapter 5, given their due praise by a harmoniously worshipping creation. It is from the standpoint of that heavenly consummation that we now see in chapters 6 and 7 the first of the series of divine judgments which continue throughout Christian history; but we are not ready to look into them until we have some conception of the heavenly criteria of divine action. So far we have learned that only the Lamb is worthy to unleash judgments upon men, since He alone has borne the judgment of God upon men's sins.

Chapter 6 deals with the opening of the seals which unleash the judgments of God progressively; but a sequence of judgments follows, namely the trumpet judgments, woes, and bowls of wrath. After seven seals are opened and their judgments poured out (6:1—8:1), there follow seven trumpet judgments (8:7—11:15), three woes (9:1—12:17), and seven bowls (or vials). The trumpet judgments from 8:7 to 11:15 are intermingled with the first two woes (9:1–12; 11:1–14); the third woe we find in 12:1–17. The judgments of the bowls are all in chapter 16.

The judgments of the seals proceed to the sixth seal, after which there is the gap of chapter 7 before the seventh seal (8:1). After four trumpet judgments (8:6–12), there is the first woe, then the fifth and sixth trumpets. Chapter 10 intervenes, followed by the second woe (11:1–14) before the seventh trumpet (11:15), and the third woe in 12:1–17.

The worthiness of the Lamb in the midst of the throne having been acknowledged by all creatures, we see the Lamb in action. *¹Now I saw when the Lamb opened one of the seven seals*; the suffering Lamb of God alone has the right to unleash judgments upon men. Those who will not have Christ as Redeemer and Saviour must face Him as Judge. *and I heard one of the four living creatures say, as with a voice of thunder, 'Come!'* The four living creatures utter in turn the word of divine command to pour out the first four judgments. They are obviously in a special relation of authority to the Almighty on the throne and to the Lamb. The outpouring of God's judgments is delegated, which suggests the supreme assurance with which God dispenses justice grounded in righteousness and grace.

²And I saw, and behold, a white horse, and its rider had a bow; and a crown was given to him, and he went out conquering and to conquer. Four horses, with their riders. Note that the four horses are derived first from Zechariah 1:8 and then 6:1–3, 7: there they are red, black, white and dappled. The question is whether this rider is Christ, or not. Some say he is, some say he is not. Undoubtedly, the rider on the white horse in 19:11 is Christ, but is Christ here one of the four horsemen, albeit the first? Certainly this judgment is not a calamity, such as war, famine or death, which follow (3–8), but the first victorious out-working of a victory over all evil already won. Does Christ lead forth the forces of judgment? It is reasonable; although some would argue that Christ would not both open the seal *and* come forth at the command of the living creature; having been 'given' a crown.

³When he opened the second seal, I heard the second living creature say, 'Come!' ⁴And out came another horse, bright red; its rider was permitted, no permission was given to the first rider! *to take peace from the earth, so that men should slay one another; and he was given a great sword.* This is war! The judgments of God are seen in the wars of men, sinful men destroying sinful men with a great sword as God ordained evil to destroy evil: see *eg* 2 Chronicles 20:23, as well as God's sovereign use of such as the Assyrians, Chaldeans, Persians, Greeks, Seleucids and Romans to subdue His own people, *eg* Jeremiah 27:6. Hitler's Germany is a modern example of this.

[5]*When he opened the third seal, I heard the third living creature say, 'Come'! And I saw, and behold, a black horse, and its rider had a balance in his hand;* [6]*and I heard what seemed to be a voice in the midst of the four living creatures saying,* note the voice of the third living creature, and then the seeming voice out of the midst of the four, *'A quart of wheat for a denarius,* a day's wages of an unskilled worker, *and three quarts of barley,* in the Middle East an inferior grain, *for a denarius; but do not harm oil and wine!'* This judgment is famine, with all the economic hardship, poverty and injustice associated with it. The most interesting and significant point here is the last statement about not harming oil and wine, which seems cynically to refer to the fact that in a suffering community the affluent leaders of the nation are generally the last to suffer hardship; *eg* see King Ahab and Obadiah in search of water for the royal horses when the people were in straits for lack of it! (1 Kings 18)

[7]*When he opened the fourth seal, I heard the voice of the fourth living creature say, 'Come!'* [8]*And I saw, and behold, a pale* (*chlorus,* chlorine, livid) *horse, and its rider's name was Death, and Hades followed him;* there is sinister suggestion here of the rapacity of death and the abode of the dead as clamouring for more death and the dead; *and they were given power* (authority) *over a fourth of the earth,* in contrast compare the fruitful fourth of the scattered seed of the Word of God (Matthew 13:3–8), *to kill with sword and with famine and with pestilence and by wild beasts of the earth.* The four horsemen have meted out their punishment upon the fourth of mankind. These are the same four means of death as in Ezekiel 14:21. Whether one sees the first three judgments as cumulative, the fourth certainly gathers up a toll of judgment, which suggests the gathering and increasing force of divine judgments in the course of Christian history: 'But understand this, that in the last days there will come times of stress...evil men...will go on from bad to worse...' (2 Tim. 3:1, 13) If we see the foregoing as descriptive of, say the

dissolution of the Roman Empire by the power of Christ, it is also repeated throughout Christian history up to the present time.

The next seal, the fifth, discloses the other side of all this, the minds of the martyr saints who have suffered death in the midst of world convulsions. ⁹*When* he opened the fifth seal, *I saw under the altar*, suggestive of the Jewish altar of burnt sacrifice, *the souls,* disembodied, *of those who had been slain for the word of God and for the witness they had borne*; see Revelation 12.11; ¹⁰*they cried out with a loud voice, 'O Sovereign Lord, holy and true, how long before thou wilt judge and avenge our blood on those who dwell upon the earth?'* These martyr souls are conscious, know what is going on in the earth (cf 1 Sam. 28; and Moses and Elijah at the Transfiguration, Luk 9:30, 31), and are apparently able to make pure and unvindictive prayer for vengeance on their destroyers, as the saints on earth, in Revelation 8:1–4, presumably were not able to do without 'much incense' derived from the Lord's high priestly prayer on their behalf. ¹¹*Then they were each given a white robe,* indication of their purity by the blood of Jesus and their witness thereto, *and told to rest* (in the sense of 'wait'?). *a little longer until the number*, of the elect, each one precisely and personally known to God, *of their fellow servants and their brethren should be complete*, which suggests the precision of our Lord's will as He purposes its accomplishment *who were to be killed as they themselves had been*. The inference is that there will be martyrs to the end of the age, which current history seems to confirm.

¹²*When he opened the sixth seal, I,* John, *looked, and behold, there was a great earthquake; and the sun became black as sackcloth, the full moon became like blood,* ¹³*and the stars of the sky fell to the earth as the fig tree sheds its winter fruit when shaken by a gale*; see Joel 2:30,31; Acts 2:19, 20; also Matthew 24:29; ¹⁴*the sky vanished like a scroll that is rolled up, and every mountain and island was removed from its place.* See Isaiah 54:10a; 2 Peter 3:7, 10, 12.

¹⁵*Then the kings of the earth and the great men and the generals and the rich and the strong,* all the categories of men who thought the world was going their way, *and every*

one, slave and free, hid in the caves and among the rocks of the mountains, [16]*calling to the mountains and rocks,* notice what they say, indicating more than fear of natural calamites, *'Fall on us and hide us,* see Isaiah 2:10, 19 *from the face of him who is seated on the throne, and from the wrath of the Lamb;* [17]*for the great day of their wrath has come, and who can stand before it?'* This is the climactic judgment of history, when the God behind the judgments of history makes Himself known in the terrors of the last judgment. Note the awful phrase, 'the wrath of the Lamb'; meekness, when righteously aroused, is terrible. See Numbers 12:3–16. The beatitude, 'Blessed are the meek, for they shall inherit the earth,' shows that meekness has a substantial reward: it cannot, therefore, be weak, however gentle and long-suffering it is; its restraint is the measure of its ultimate judgment and vindication. The Lamb is the Lion!

CHAPTER SEVEN

The Redeemed
7:1–17

This chapter has been called an interlude, but it is, rather, a turning to the positive and blessed side of judgment (cf 6:9–11) for relief, or a drawing back the dark curtain of judgment to remind us that judgment serves salvation, not salvation judgment: see the proper order and priority of these two in, *eg* Romans 9:22, 23. The first verses of chapter 7 describe in graphic terms the divine restraint of natural calamities in respect of the elect, so that no satanically precipitated human disaster can interfere with their sealing unto God; see John 6:27; 2 Corinthians 1:22; Ephesians 1:13; 4:30.

¹*After this I saw four angels standing at the four corners of the earth,* this is universal, *holding back the four winds of the earth,* compare these with Zechariah 6:1–6, especially verse 5, *that no wind might blow on earth or sea or against any tree.* These control the entire movements of human history between the two comings of Christ.

²*Then I saw another angel ascend from the rising of the sun,* The four corners of the earth having been mentioned, the direction of this executive angel is noted. Why from the east? Is it as simple as that the Holy Land, the land of the tribes about to be enumerated was east of John in Patmos? Or is the emphasis upon the sun of God's glory arising upon a dark world to seal the Lord's own? *with the seal of the living God, and he called with a loud voice to the four angels who had been given power,* the word 'power' is not in the original,

to harm earth and sea, ³*saying, 'Do not harm the earth or the sea or the trees, till we have sealed the servants of our God upon their foreheads.'* The seal marks owernship, see Revelation 9:4; 14:1; 22:4; Ephesians 1:13. This thought contains the blessed truth that before the forces of judgment are permitted their exercise, God seals His chosen, so that they are as safe amidst the satanically inspired turmoil of earth as if they were already in God's heaven. 'Yes, I to the end shall endure, As sure as the earnest is given; More happy, but not more secure, The glorified spirits in heaven.' (Toplady) Not only so: although in history many of God's judgments are executed for Him by His enemies (consider the mighty pagan nations which afflicted Israel for her sins), ultimate judgment is in the hands of God Himself and His angels. This is important, to assure us that all God's judgments are just and perfect, whether executed directly by His command or by His ordained permissions of evil.

⁴*And I heard the number of the sealed, a hundred and forty-thousand sealed, out of every tribe of the sons of Israel,* ⁵*twelve thousand sealed out of the tribe of Judah, twelve thousand of the tribe of Reuben, twelve thousand of the tribe of Gad,* ⁶*twelve thousand of the tribe of Asher, twelve thousand of the tribe of Naphtali, twelve thousand of the tribe of Manasseh,* ⁷*twelve thousand of the tribe of Simeon, twelve thousand of the tribe of Levi, twelve thousand of the tribe of Issachar,* ⁸*twelve thousand of the tribe of Zebulun, twelve thousand of the tribe of Joseph, twelve thousand sealed out of the tribe of Benjamin.*

Dan is excluded, and Joseph is divided in two, Manasseh and Ephraim (called here, Joseph). Why is Dan excluded? It is suggested, from Judges 18:30, 31, that they did not deserve to be included on account of their idolatry—not to speak of presuming on the prerogative of the priestly tribe. We see what such idolatry led to in 1 Kings 12:19, when the ten tribes departed from foolish Rehoboam (son of Solomon). Morris suggests that Dan was omitted also because 'antichrist would arise from this tribe'; and a footnote; 'This view is put forward by Irenaeus who bases it on the words, 'The snorting of his horses was heard from Dan' (Jer. 8:16). Swete cites Hippolytus: 'As the Christ was born of the tribe of

Judah so the Antichrist will be born of the tribe of Dan.' Satan is said to be this tribe's prince. Dan's bad reputation may be quite old, for this tribe (along with Zebulun) is omitted from the genealogies in the early chapters of 1 Chronicles.' (Morris, p.115).

Note also that the order of the tribes here is different from that in every other Scripture. The number 144,000, which arithmetically-minded scholars love to play with in multiples of 3, 4, 10 and 12, may be regarded as the true Israel of God, the entire church militant (Old Testament and New). The sealing for protection indicates that they are upon the earth and exposed to danger, yet safe, see Ephesians 1:13, 14. By contrast, in the next verse (9) we have the picture of the whole church triumphant in heaven, and with this glorious scene, says Hendriksen, the section (chapters 4 to 7) and the dispensation end with the church glorified. Here without doubt we may with confidence feast our minds and hearts on the ultimate consummation.

⁹*After this I looked, and behold, a great multitude which no man could number, from all tribes and peoples and tongues, standing before the throne before the Lamb, clothed in white robes, with palm branches in their hands,* ¹⁰*and crying out with a loud voice,* here is complete abandonment to the climax of all ages, *'Salvation belongs to our God who sits upon the throne, and to the Lamb!'* The innumerable company, standing in white robes with palm branches, redolent of our Lord's triumphant entry into Jerusalem, cry with loud voices and proclaim the total self-giving of the saints to this acknowledgement. This may well represent to us the end which the Almighty God has in view in redeeming us, that we might pour ourselves out in utter worship of God and the Lamb. For such is the end of our being, what we were made for; our fullest, most blessed, God-pleasing employment. Note, before we read verse 11, that it is the saints who 'call the tune', for they are God's elite; the angelic orders then respond.

¹¹*And all the angels stood round the throne and round the elders and the four living creatures, and they fell on their faces,* even the elect angels (1 Tim. 5:21) are not fit to stand before God, *before the throne and worshipped God,* ¹²*saying,*

'Amen! Blessing and glory and wisdom and thanksgiving and honour and power and might, note the sevenfold ascription and compare it with 5:12, *be to our God for ever and ever! Amen.'*

From the aesthetic point of view there follows at verse 13 a touching change from the universal to the particular. It is as if a great symphony, which had been pealing forth the most glorious music, chose to end the work with a coda of pathos and haunting beauty. What in this case would be the 'haunting' note? Surely the former 'great tribulation' whence these radiant saints were redeemed.

¹³Then one of the elders addressed me, saying, 'Who are these, clothed in white robes, and whence have they come?' *¹⁴I,* John, *said to him, 'Sir, you know.'* John's deference is not necessarily on account of ignorance, but respect, see 19:10; 22:8. *And he said to me, 'These are they who have come out of the great tribulation*; What is the 'great tribulation'? Surely, the enmity of unbelieving earth and hell; see chapter 6, and note the fact of the sealing for protection. *they have washed their robes and made them white in the blood of the Lamb.* This form of words justifies the evangelical hymns which sing of being 'washed in the blood of the Lamb'. The imagery is scriptural, whether men deride it or not. It is the blood of death, the holy, sinless death of the God/Man, which makes black hearts clean and gloriously white. See Isaiah 1:18; 1 Corinthians 6:11; Hebrews 9:14. *¹⁵Therefore are they*, that is why they are, *before the throne of God*, for that is where such perfect cleansing takes guilty sinners, *and serve him day and night within his temple*; there is no intermission; it is a perpetual activity because it is completely engaging and satisfying; *and he who sits upon the throne will shelter* spread his tent over *them with his presence.'* What a beautiful expression! The thought of the Shekinah, that is the hovering, radiant presence of God, takes us back to Israel's experience in the wilderness; but, also, directly to the shelter of the blood upon the lintel of the door of the houses of Israel on the dread night of Passover. 'When I see the blood, I will pass over you, and no plague shall fall upon you to destroy you, when I smite the land of Egypt.' (Exod. 12:13) That is on the negative, protective side.

[16]*"They shall hunger no more, neither thirst any more*; We are reminded of Israel in the wilderness experiencing hunger and thirst, not only in Sinai, but later in other lands of their captivity, but these have ceased (see Is. 49:10a), for our Lord's blessed words in the beatitude (Matt. 5:6) are for ever and perfectly fulfilled; 'those who hunger and thirst for righteousness' are 'satisfied'. *the sun shall not strike them, nor any scorching heat.* See Psalm 121:5–6 and Isaiah 49:10b. [17]*for the Lamb,* an exquisite and tender touch! *in the midst of the throne will be their shepherd,* 'The Lord is my shepherd, I shall not want', *and he will guide them to springs of living water;* see Exodus 15:27; 17:6; Numbers 20:11; 2 Samuel 23:15; Isaiah 49:10c; John 4:7–14; 7:37–39; Revelation 22:1–2; *and God will wipe away every tear from their eyes.'* See Isaiah 25:8–9; 35:10. These scriptural references, among the most significant in relation to these words, indicate that what the saints now enjoy in God's presence is what He has been promising them since man went astray. Perhaps the chief impression of this last superb passage of the section is of satisfaction, where formerly there was anguish and deprivation. Jesus satisfies!

CHAPTER EIGHT

The Warning Trumpets
8:1-13

Chapter 8 begins with a seeming ending, which turns out to be a new beginning, that of the third section of the epistle (chapters 8–11), which covers again the ground between the first and second comings of Christ. The opening of the seventh and last seal leads to the sounding of the seven trumpets.

¹*When the Lamb opened the seventh seal, there was silence in heaven for about half an hour.* The silence suggests awe and worship (see Hab. 2:20; Zeph. 1:7; Zech 2:13) as John turns from the praises of the redeemed and glorified throng to the prayers of the suffering saints on earth.

²*Then I saw the seven angels who stand before God*, seven angels are mentioned also in 8:6; 15:1, 6; 16:1; 17:1; 21:9: 1 Enoch 20:1–8 ventures to give their names and offices; Uriel, over the world and Tartarus (hell); Raphael, over the spirits of men; Raguel, who takes vengeance on the world of luminaries; Michael, over the 'best part of mankind and over chaos'; Saraqâêl, over 'the spirits who sin in spirit'; Gabriel, over Paradise and the serpents and cherubim; Remiel, 'whom God set over those who rise': *and seven trumpets were given to them.* On the view of the seven sections of Revelation covering the same general ground between the two comings of Christ, the opening of the seven seals (chapter 6) is synchronous with the sounding of the seven trumpets.

³*And another angel came and stood at the altar with a golden censer; and he was given much incense to mingle with the prayers of all the saints upon the golden altar before the*

67

throne; ⁴*and the smoke of the incense rose with the prayers of the saints from the hand of the angel before God.* Compare with Revelation 5:8, and with 6:9–11 where the disembodied souls of martyr saints cry for vengeance on their persecutors. In that perfect state they do so safely without ungodly vindictiveness, but saints on earth are still susceptible to carnal vengefulness, so that their imperfect prayers must needs be mingled with incense of the perfect intercessory prayers of their heavenly High Priest, the Lord Jesus Christ, before they are acceptable at the throne of heavenly grace and judgment. See Hebrews 2:10; 4:14–16; 5:2, 7–9. As the Lord Jesus Christ's heavenly intercession on our behalf is offered on the ground of His own prayers during His passion 'with strong crying and tears', our prayers to Him must also be offered within the same perfect intercession. Stated simply, this means that the only prayers of sinful saints to reach the ears of God in heaven are those made within the redeeming intercession of Jesus Christ, since He alone is acceptable to God, on His own behalf, and on ours. See John chapter 17.

> And now, O Father, mindful of the
>   love
> That bought us, once for all, on
>   Calvary's Tree,
> And having with us Him that pleads
>   above,
> We here are present, we here spread
>   forth to Thee
> That only offering perfect in Thine
>   eyes,
> The one true, pure, immortal
>   sacrifice.
>
> Look, Father, look on His anointed
>   face,
> And only look on us as found in
>   Him.
>
> (William Bright)

⁵*Then the angel took the censer and filled it with fire from the altar and threw in on the earth; and there were peals of*

thunder, loud noises, flashes of lightning, and an earthquake. This means that the prayers of saints still suffering on earth are for judgment, or include prayers for judgment. The judgments which afflict the earth during man's probation, following the coming of Christ, are thus now introduced; see Ezekiel 10;2.

⁶*Now the seven angels who had the seven trumpets made ready to blow them.* ⁷*The first angel blew his trumpet, and there followed hail and fire, mixed with blood, which fell on the earth; and a third of the earth was burnt up, and a third of the trees were burnt up, and all green grass was burnt up.* This verse is quoted in a modern scientific pamphlet on pollution! The first judgment corresponds to the seven plagues of Egypt (Exod. 7:20ff.) The trumpet, of course, warns (Ezek. 33:3). These judgments must be regarded as warnings of worse things to follow on earth if men do not repent.

But God is perpetually judging His creatures, through nature and the elements. The strong reaction of sentimentalists to this only underlines the grim reality of the inexorable holiness of God which must take its vindicatory toll on those who spurn His mercy and grace. The reference to the 'third' (see Zech. 13:8–9) indicates the selectiveness of divine judgment on grounds which can only be according to His righteous knowledge.

⁸*The second angel blew his trumpet, and something like a great mountain, burning with fire, was thrown into the sea;* ⁹*and a third of the sea became blood, a third of the living creatures in the sea died, and a third of the ships were destroyed.* The idea of the burning mountain probably comes from 1 Enoch 18:13; 21:3; 108:4. (This apocalyptic, apocryphal book may be consulted for other reasons, *eg* Jude 14–16.) There is also reference to the first Egyptian plague, the sea turning into blood (Exod. 7:20; Ps 78:44). For the destruction of the fish of the sea, see Zephaniah 1:3. See also the psalmist's refuge from these horrors (Ps. 46:1, 2).

¹⁰*The third angel blew his trumpet, and a great star fell from heaven, blazing like a torch, and it fell on a third of the rivers and on the fountain of water.* ¹¹*The name of the star is Wormwood. A third of the waters became wormwood, and*

many died of the water, because it was made bitter. The
blazing star falling out of heaven is probably a reference to
Satan falling like lightning (see Luke 10:18), for that accur-
ately describes his situation following Christ's victory on
the cross. We have a further reference to this in Revelation
12:9. The reference to the falling of the star, however, could
go back to the fall of angels (or demon-inspired men)
recorded in Genesis 6:1–2, taken along with 1 Peter 3:19–
20; 2 Peter 2:4; Jude 6 (see also 1 Enoch chapters 6–11); or it
may refer to the primeval casting down of Lucifer, see
Ezekiel 28:12–19; Isaiah 14:12–19. As to Wormwood, see
Jeremiah 9:15; 23:15; Lamentations 3:15, 19; Amos 5:7;
6:12; also Deuteronomy 29:18–19 and Proverbs 5:4. The
obnoxious nature of satanic and demonic influences upon
the earth is vividly portrayed. We could doubt that such
grim spiritual realities underlie the calamitous things
which take place on earth?

[12]*The fourth angel blew his trumpet, and a third of the sun
was struck, and a third of the moon, and a third of the stars,
so that a third of their light was darkened; a third of the day
was kept from shining, and likewise a third of the night.* This
is a particularly difficult verse, since it would be hard to
take it metaphorically in a series describing natural judgments. See Amos 8:9. These events can refer only to eclipses
and such other solar, lunar and astral occurrences as point
to disorders in the cosmic spheres reacting to human
wickedness upon earth, but which thus far ('third') are
partial. See the ninth plague, Exodus 10:21–23, and
Matthew 24:29; Mark 13:24; Luke 23:45.

[13]*Then I looked, and I heard an eagle crying with a loud
voice, as it flew in midheaven, 'Woe, woe, woe to those who
dwell on the earth, at the blasts of the other trumpets which
the three angels are about to blow!'* This verse, with its eagle
as a bird of prey (Matt. 24:28), indicates that the results of
the first three warning trumpets have only begun to afflict
the people on earth (the judgments in chapter 8 are
physical), but worse is to come (those of chapter 9 are
spiritual) and in the form of three 'woes', following the
blasts of the fifth, sixth and seventh trumpets. We are
launched immediately into these in the following chapter.

CHAPTER NINE

The First Woe
9:1-21

¹And the fifth angel blew his trumpet, and I saw a star fallen from heaven to earth, and he was given the key of the shaft of the bottomless pit; Great controversy surrounds who this 'he' is: scholarly opinions range from the one extreme of Satan, to the other of an angel or man, or even our Lord Himself. Whether 'he' is Satan, or one of his fallen angelic agents, we need not fear to ascribe evil power or personality to him, because all such powers and beings are, happily, under the control of the Almighty. We know that ultimately God is the destroying power (Matt. 10:28), but often in history He employs evil itself (although He is implacably opposed to it) to do His 'strange' work of judgment. Yet it is never the will of evil agents to help God, but rather hinder Him. But the Almighty has so built His universe that evil cannot but help Him. The more it tries to work against Him, the more He uses its evil for good. It does not seem to have the spiritual intelligence to desist. Perhaps it does know that it is serving God, but is unable to stop its evil career!

²he opened the shaft of the bottomless pit, and from the shaft rose smoke like the smoke of a great furnace, and the sun and the air were darkened with the smoke from the shaft. The 'bottomless pit' is the abyss of Luke 8:31 (as also Rom. 10:7; Rev. 9:11; 11:7; 17:8; 20:1, 3); and is, says Charles, 'the *preliminary* place of punishment of the fallen angels, of demons, of the Beast, and the false Prophet, and the prison one thousand years of Satan.' *(The International Critical*

Commentary, p.239) It may also be the same prison as in 1
Peter 3:19, 20; see also Genesis 6:1–2; 2 Peter 2;4; Jude 6;
and 1 Enoch chapters 21–22.

³*Then from the smoke came locusts on the earth, and they
were given power like the power of scorpions of the earth;* for
'smoke' see Genesis 19:28, concerning Sodom; the eighth
plague of locusts, Exodus 10:4–15; the book of Joel; and
consider the effects of a plague of locusts upon every green
thing; ⁴*they were told not to harm the grass of the earth or any
green growth or any tree, but only those of mankind who have
not the seal of God upon their foreheads;* Whatever direct or
indirect effect the judgments have upon the chosen and
faithful following the first three trumpets, they are
certainly protected from the upsurge of demonic hordes. It
follows, therefore, that the command forbidding hurt to
those with the seal of God upon their foreheads must come
from God Himself, or from His authority, see 7:1–8. ⁵*they
were allowed to torture them,* those on the earth not sealed,
*for five months, but not to kill them, and their torture was like
the torture of a scorpion, when it stings a man.* Five months
may suggest an incomplete, temporary affliction, but the
fact that a scorpion sting is 'rarely fatal' (Morris) indicates
the impossibility of finding relief from it while it lasts. This
suggest the relentlessness of evil once it is let loose.

⁶*And in those days men will seek death and will not find it;
they will long to die, and death will fly* from them. The desire
for death is expressed in Jeremiah 8:3 (see also Ecclesiastes
4:2–3), but only in Job 3:21 do we find anything as
intolerable as the desire to seek death and not find it. What
can it mean? In view of the opportunity to repent which is
afforded even such tormented survivors (vv.20–21), is it not
likely that the power which prevented them from dying was
God's power, so that they were caught between the cross
purposes of the Lord and His foe?

⁷*In appearance the locusts were like horses arrayed for
battle; on their heads were what looked like crowns of gold;
their faces were like human faces,* ⁸*their hair like women's
hair, and their teeth like lion's teeth;* For the appearance like
horses, see Joel 2:4; Job 39:20a; and for 'lions' teeth', Joel
1:6: the combination of human and animal qualities subtly

suggests horrid demonic beings; whereas the four different varieties of locusts in Joel 1:4 (there are seven different names for locusts in the Old Testament and more in Hebrew) suggest very different sorts of demons. It is said that close-up photographs of some of these locusts show their remarkable similarities to the descriptions here. It is also not insignificant that degraded 'pop' idols contrive to make themselves look increasingly like savages, and even animals! *9they had scales like iron breastplates, and the noise of their wings was like the noise of many chariots with horses rushing into battle.* As to the noise, see Joel 2:5, 10. *They have tails like scorpions, and stings, and their power of hurting men for five months lies in their tails.* An Arab from Basra describes them thus: 'With the head of a horse, the breast of a lion, feet of a camel, the body of a snake, the tail of a scorpion, its antènnae like the hair of a maiden.'

11They have as king over them the angel of the bottomless pit; his name in Hebrew is Abaddon, and in Greek he is called Apollyon. Is there here a derogatory allusion to Apollo? The locusts in Proverbs 30:27 'have no king, yet all of them march in rank': this is also true of other flying creatures in full flight, on migration, or searching for food. It is not true that the demonic world is without leadership, see Matthew 25:41; 2 Corinthians 12:7; Revelation 12:9. Abaddon means destruction (see Job 26:6; 28:22; Ps. 88:11; Prov. 15:11); and Apollyon, Destroyer.

12The first woe has passed; behold, two woes are still to come. These three woes are of a more spiritual nature (although described in grotesque physical terms) than the first four warning judgments (chapter 8); this appears more clearly in the second woe (chapter 9:13–21) and in the third (chapter 11:15–19).

13Then the sixth angel blew his trumpet, and I heard a voice from the four horns of the golden altar before God, the 'golden altar' in the Jewish tabernacle and temple was the altar of incense (prayer) within the holy place: this would seem not unrelated to the cries for vengeance, see 6:9–11; 8:1–15; *14saying to the sixth angel who had the trumpet, 'Release the four angels who are bound at the great river Euphrates.'* The river Euphrates was the limit of the

Promised Land (Gen. 15:18; Deut. 1:7; Josh. 1:4; see also Rev. 16:12). *15So the four angels were released, who had been held ready for the hour, the day, the month, and the year, to kill a third of mankind.* Note the divine meticulousness and punctuality.

16The number of the troops of cavalry was twice ten thousand times ten thousand; see Psalm 68:17; *I heard their number.* We must remember that this huge number, two hundred million, refers to demon spirits (compare possibly two thousand demons inhabiting the demoniac of Gadara). Note also the divine control over such dreadful forces of evil as, *eg* Job. 1:12a; 2:6; Zechariah 3:1–4a. What are these, and whence are they? It would be easy to associate them with hordes of Assyrians and Babylonians who came down upon hapless Israel and Judah in Old Testament days, but Charles thinks they represent vast incursions of 'angels of punishment' upon the wicked world, which punishment is familiar in apocalyptic literature, *eg* 1 Enoch 40:7; 53:3; 56:1; 62:11; 63:1; 66:1.

17And this was how I saw the horses in my vision; the riders wore breastplates the colour of fire and of sapphire and of sulphur, and the heads of the horses were like lions' heads, and fire and smoke and sulphur issued from their mouths. *18By these three plagues*, keep in mind that these are demonic, and their effects are therefore bound to be more subtle than if they were natural and physical, *a third of mankind was killed, by the fire and smoke and sulphur issuing from their mouths.* The only way to understand these mysteries is to try to transpose what they describe from the natural realm to that of the spiritual and demonic. *19For the power of the horses is in their mouths and in their tails; their tails are like serpents, with heads, and by means of them they wound.* Keeping firmly in mind that this is spiritual and demonic, as stated, the effects are therefore bound to be in the realm of the mental and psychological rather than the physical, although the physical is also bound to be affected.

20The rest of mankind, who were not killed by these plagues, did not repent of the works of their hands nor give up worshipping demons and idols of gold and silver and bronze and stone and wood, which cannot either see or hear or walk [21]*nor did they repent of their murders or their sorceries or their immorality or their thefts.* It is a fearful fact that not all the horrors described are able to turn the rest of mankind from their hell-bent path. They are sold to do evil, and either see nothing wrong in their way of life, or, if they are shocked at the grotesque effects wrought by demonic spirits on people as they die terrible deaths, attribute them to other causes. The powers of Satan have gripped them, to prevent any possibility of the light of truth penetrating their darkened minds; they are already lost, before death! See also chapter 16:11, 21; and Romans 1:18ff.

Here the close association of demons and idols is more than interesting: a sinister implication underlies the lifelessness of the idols of gold, silver, bronze, stone and wood. 1 Kings 18:26–29; Psalms 115:4–8; 135:15–18; Isaiah 44:9–20; Daniel 5:23; 1 Corinthians 10:19–21, all bring out that behind lifeless idols lie seductive demon spirits, who mesmerise and captivate their worshippers, so that they associate the spirits animating and activating them in their orgies with the images. These experiences are still common in the East, and especially in Tibet and Nepal.

Of the four categories of wickedness mentioned, 'sorceries' is particularly interesting, since the Greek word, *pharmakeia*, suggests drugs, and poisoning, as well as enchantments. Soutar in his Lexicon says of the word, 'it refers to the practice of drugging; hence, especially from the use of mysterious liquids, sorcery, witchcraft, inextricably combined with idolatry.' (Soutar, p.39) Immorality and theft would inevitably issue from such evil involvement.

As to the hardening of men's hearts, we see the same process in less spectacular terms in Isaiah 6:9–11 (Matt. 13:10–16); and in Matthew chapter 23. How we should hate evil! See Psalms 97:10; 139:21; Proverbs 8:13; Ecclesiastes 3:8; Amos 5:15.

CHAPTER TEN

The Little Scroll
10:1–11

We have seen in the course of chapters 8 and 9 a progression of judgment throughout the Christian ages, from physical to psychological and spiritual. Daniel chapter 12 should be read in conjuction with this chapter since much of its imagery derives from it. Daniel chapter 12 looks beyond the Babylonian captivity to the persecution of the Jews under Antiochus Ephiphanes (167 BC) to the early persecutions of the Church by Nero in the first century right through to those of the third century. In chapter 10 there seems to be an interruption: Morris calls it an 'interlude'. It is like the 'breaking' of the headlong rush of the last movement of a symphony in order to reassemble the hearer's powers of concentration for the grand ending. The description of the mighty angel suggests the universal drama about to be enacted.

¹Then I saw another mighty angel coming down from heaven wrapped in a cloud, with a rainbow over his head, and his face was like the sun, and his legs like pillars of fire. The picture is so transcendant that it appears to portray the Lord Himself, in grace (the sun, and the rainbow), and in judgment (the cloud, and the pillars of fire). Not so: but the angel undoubtedly represents the Lord of the universe in all His glory. *²He had a little scroll open in his hand. And he set his right foot on the sea, and his left foot on the land,* see Psalm 60:8, describing the divine Colossus, *³and called out with a loud voice, like a lion roaring; when he called out, the*

76

seven thunders sounded. But no lightning, observes one, since what the thunder says it is not permitted to speak.

⁴*And when the seven thunders had sounded,* see Psalm 29, the seven-fold thunderous 'voice of the Lord', *I was about to write, but I heard a voice from heaven saying, 'Seal up what the seven thunders have said, and do not write it down.'* See Isaiah 8:16; Daniel 12:4; 2 Corinthians 12:4. The meaning thus far, which should be taken as broadly as possible to avoid eccentricities of interpretation, seems to be that there are depths of mystery, especially of judgment which are not ours to know. Instead we are to be subdued before the vastness of the unknown purposes of God, and await the dire as well as the glorious outcome of holy history with holy fear, total humility and bated breath. The interruption of John in his act of writing down what had transpired is therefore not to be taken as symbolising delay (that is specifically denied), but pause for wonderment. This is confirmed by the statement now made by the angel.

⁵*And the angel whom I saw standing on sea and land lifted up his right hand to heaven* ⁶*and swore by him who lives for ever and ever, who created heaven and what is in it, and the sea and what is in it, that there should be no more delay,* ⁷*but that in the days of the trumpet call* of warning *to be sounded by the seventh angel, the mystery of God, as he announced to his servants the prophets, should be fulfilled.* Take the phrase, 'no more delay', in conjuction with the angel's command to John not to write what he had heard in the seven thunders, as if to say, 'Hold, but not for long.' It may also be understood as part of the Lord's general warning to His people not to assume that God is inactive because everything does not happen at once! The drama of the whole passage is lost if the angel's command to John to 'Seal up...is regarded as other than a temporary restraint; cf the relativity of time in 2 Peter 3:8–10a.

The 'mystery of God' is elemental: it is an all-embracing secret of God, only to be made known in the event, although more than adumbrated already in the revelations of holy history; see Amos 3:7; 1 Peter 1:10–12. On the one hand, the mystery to be fulfilled would be God's full and satisfying answer to all His children's bewildered questions, particularly about His permissions of evil; but more roundly and positively it would include the outworkings of the complexities of His will respecting Jews and Gentiles in His one church; see Romans chapters 9–11. Meantime, the mystery which was revealed to John through the seven thunders, and which appears to be inscribed in the little scroll, is to be digested by John, with bitter result, and accompanied with a word of prophetic command.

⁸Then the voice which I had heard from heaven spoke to me again, saying, 'Go, take the scroll which is open in the hand of the angel who is standing on the sea and on the land.' ⁹So I went to the angel and told him to give me the little scroll; and he said to me, 'Take it and eat; it will be bitter to your stomach, but sweet as honey in your mouth.; ¹⁰And I took the little scroll from the hand of the angel and ate it; it was sweet as honey in my mouth, but when I had eaten it my stomach was made bitter. ¹¹And I was told, 'You must again prophesy about many peoples and nations and tongues and kings.'

The fact that the result of eating the scroll is first sweet, then bitter indicates that the Lord is revealing to John (and to us), that while it is sweet for us as His servants to receive His word, the outcome of that Word will be bitter for the Lord's servants, when they speak it, but far worse for the world. This is clear from the Lord's commissions to His chosen prophets, mentioned above: see Isaiah 6:9; Jeremiah 1:7, 8, 17–19, 15:15–17; Ezekiel 3:1–3, 14, 15. How are we to take this in practical application? Chapter 11 will show; but in general it cannot mean that the sweetness of God's Word is temporary and that it then becomes sour, but rather that the Lord's presence with us in His Word in any experience of life enables us to bear the bitterness associated with its execution. See Psalm 119:41–48, especially v.46.

CHAPTER ELEVEN

The Two Witnesses
11:1–19

This chapter illustrates the 'mystery of God' in chapter 10, whose theme is the bitter experience of the church in the world; see 2 Corinthians 4:3, 4.

¹*Then I was given a measuring rod like a staff, and I was told: 'Rise and measure the temple of God and the altar and those who worship there,* ²*but do not measure the court outside the temple; leave that out, for it is given over to the nations, and they will trample over the holy city,* see Isaiah 63:18; Daniel 8:13; Luke 21:24, *for forty-two months.'*

The chapter arouses great controversy, but verses 1 and 2 are clear enough. They define the true church as distinct from Christendom. The symbolism is undoubtedly taken from Herod's temple, and is therefore not to be taken literally. The true church is measured and defined for preservation; not that she may not suffer, but she cannot perish; whereas wordly Christendom is the prey of every ungodly force, and has no power to withstand evil encroachments; it will be trampled all over. This has been sufficiently true throughout the ages not to require proof beyond the facts of history.

The period 'forty-two months' is, of coure, equal to 'one thousand two hundred and sixty days (see v.3 and 12:6); and 'a time, and times, and half a time', three and a half years (see 12:14): Daniel 7:25; 12:7. It represents 'the present Gospel age' (Hendriksen). The idea derives from the three years' drought pronounced by Elijah (1 Kings 17:1) and

79

called 'three years and six months' by James (5:17). It was a period of judgment on Israel for the sins of Ahab and Jezebel.

³*'And I will grant my two witnesses power to prophesy for one thousand two hundred and sixty days, clothed in sackcloth.'* The great question is: Who are the two witnesses? But first note that during this period of the gospel age, the two witnesses will be given 'power to prophesy', but they will be clothed in sackcloth', which means that they mourn the sins of both Christendom and the heathen world. Who are the two witnesses who go out into the world with the Lord's prophetic word? They have been variously identified with Moses and Elijah, Elijah and Elisha, and Enoch and Elijah (both of whom ascended to heaven without dying); they have been equated with the Law and the Prophets, the Law and the Gospel, and even the Old and New Testaments. It is idle to identify them with specific characters; better to try to find their true symbolism. Morris suggests that the number two, 'may stand for the adequacy of testimony' (Deut. 17:6), which, in terms of gospel witnessing, agrees with Luke 10:1, where we read that the Lord sent His disciples out 'two by two'. We therefore accept them as two witnesses representing all those who through the ages have faithfully and fearlessly witnessed to Christ and have 'loved not their lives even unto death' (12:11), but perhaps particularly towards the end of the age. They are now described in other symbolic terms.

⁴*These are the two olive trees and the two lampstands which stand before the Lord of the earth.* This is taken from Zechariah chapter 4: see especially verse 3, borrowing the picture of the lampstand of pure gold in the tabernacle; see Exodus 25:31–40; 27:20, 21; 37:17–24. The oil stands for the Holy Spirit ministering Christ ('the light of the world', John 9:5; 12:46) flowing from the trees to the lamp in perpetual supply. This is 'before the Lord of the earth', which means in his sight, by His direction and for His purposes, which is important in view of what follows about those who would harm his 'lamps' or witnesses. (Jesus said, 'You are the light of the world'; Matt. 5:14).

⁵*And if any one would harm them, fire pours from their*

mouth and consumes their foes; if any one would harm them, thus he is doomed to be killed. This is expressed in lurid terms, but it comes from Jeremiah 5:14, and refers primarily to that timid prophet. It does not mean, of course, that the Lord's servants have the right to stalk around, breathing fire upon all who initially resist or oppose them (*cf* Luke 9:51–56—including marginal references in RSV!), but it certainly means that prophetic condemnations (especially of two prophets agreeing) in the name of the Lord are effective; see Matthew 18:15– 20. See also the clear account of the condemnation of Ananias and Sapphira (Acts 5:1–11). 11).

⁶*They have power* (authority) *to shut the sky, that no rain may fall during the days of their prophesying, and they have power* (authority) *over the waters to turn them into blood, and to smite the earth with every plague, as they desire.* The first allusion is to Elijah (1 Kings 17:1; Jas. 5:17); the others to the plagues of Egypt (Exodus chs. 7–12). These instances of judgment vested in the Lord's servants are of particular interest and importance in view of their temptation to carnal vindictiveness. The cry for vengeance in Revelation 6:9–11 is made, as we have seen, by disembodied souls who are not tempted to carnal vengeance. Saints on earth may also cry (Rev. 3.1–5), but their prayers must be mingled with the incense of Christ's perfect prayers to keep them pure. We may be sure that in these circumstances, neither Moses, nor Elijah, nor Jeremiah, nor any Spirit-inspired servant of God would act capriciously or wantonly, but solemnly, and in the fear of God. Certainly, authority over the powers of nature is promised us by Christ (see Mark 11:23, 24); but here they are directed towards punitive ends. These are part of the tremendous powers mediated to Christ's church, for blessing or otherwise, which a prayerless church never suspects, let alone exercises.

⁷*And when they have finished their testimony, the beast that ascends from the bottomless pit will make war upon them* (Dan. 7.21) *and conquer them and kill them,* ⁸*and their dead bodies will lie in the street of the great city which is allegorically* (margin, spiritually) *called Sodom* (Isa. 1:9; Ezek. 16.46, 55), *and* Egypt (Wisdom 29:14), *where their*

Lord was crucified. Although in a sensible symbolic interpretation of the two witnesses their testimony would
conclude towards the end of the gospel age, there is perhaps
room for interpretations of the verse which apply it to any
witnesses who are 'immortal until their work is done'. This
surely explains the unhappy earthly end of many of God's
doughty warriors–not to be confused with the backsliding in
old age of such as Noah, David and Solomon.

The picture of the dead bodies of the witnesses spread-
eagled in the street of the ungodly city for all the worldly to
see is particularly revolting, but it is surely the inevitable
result of following Him who calls us to share (within the
categories given us) His 'horrible' death. The world gloats
over this, and will do so increasingly (contrast Romans chs.
9—11) as gospel witness is progressively silenced and
Christ's church trampled under foot. How this apostasy is to
be integrated prophetically with the glowing picture of
movements of the Spirit involving Jews and Gentiles
towards the end of the age, as elicited by Iain Murray from
Puritan writers in *The Puritan Hope*, we may not know;
but that it has to be so integrated, and, equally biblically,
there can be no doubt.

[9]*For three days and a half,* not to be confused with three
and a half years (*cf* 11.2–3; 12:6, 14;; 13:5), *men from the
peoples and tribes and tongues and nations gaze at their dead
bodies and refuse to let them be placed in a tomb,* [10]*and those
who dwell on the earth will rejoice over them and make merry
and exchange presents, because these two prophets had been
a torment to those who dwell on the earth.* The 'three days
and a half' represent the short sharp burst of final persecution towards the end of the age; whereas the 'three and a half
years' derive from the reference in James 5;17 to the testing
time of drought in Elijah's day, which lasted for three years
and six months. This period, whether expressed in terms of
years, months, times or days, or even a thousand years, is
the time between Christ's first and second comings and is a
time of testing for His people. The 'three days and a half', on
the other hand, represent the 'little' testing of the saints
towards the end of the age, elsewhere called the fnal
'apostasy' (2 Thess. 2:3; 'rebellion', RSV). Hendriksen refers

to Matthew 24:22, concerning the shortened time of the tribulation: see also Revelation 20:7–9, which is the final section of the book (chapters 20—22), describing the 'little' time in terms of Satan's brief release before the final judgment. It is a time when witness to Christ will appear to cease on earth; see Luke 18:8b (*cf* Luke 17:22–37; also 2 Thess. 2;1–12; Matt. 24:9–13; 1 Tim. 4:1–3; 2 Pet. 3:17; 1 John 2:18; 4:3.

The above scriptural references meet the conditions prevailing when the generality of peoples look not only with contempt but with gloating and glee upon the dead bodies of the witnesses lying in the streets, and refuse them burial. Not only so, but they make a festival of their destruction, 'because these two prophets had been a torment to those who dwell on the earth.' What torment? It has been represented already in the descriptions of the judgments of the seals, the warning trumpets, and the first woe. So they rejoice and send each other presents (as is now done at Christmas, and as in other circumstances the Jews did in Esther's day [9:22]. The prospect of such hatred of Christians is brought out by our Lord in John 15:18–22; 16:2–4.

[11]*But after the three and a half days, a breath of life from God entered them, and they stood up on their feet, and great fear fell on those who saw them.* This further reversal of fortunes is perhaps most surprising of all; but, since the three and a half days are over, we may regard what is described as belonging to the fruits of our Lord's coming in power and glory. Then Christ's church, at the end of her tribulation, is vindicated before the eyes of the unbelieving and persecuting world as enjoying God's special care, and as holding the key to the drama of redemption. The fear expressed is but the beginning of the eternal sorrows of those who have ill-used the saints.

[12]*Then they heard a loud voice from heaven saying to them, 'Come up hither!' And in the sight of their foes they went up to heaven in a cloud.* This public vindication and rapture deny the alleged 'secret' rapture. [13]*And at that hour there was a great earthquake, and a tenth of the city fell; seven thousand people were killed in the earthquake, cf* Matthew 27:51–54; 28:2, *and the rest were terrified and gave glory to the God of*

heaven. All is described in terms of the 'great city', variously called Sodom, Egypt, Jerusalem and (later) Babylon; but it describes universal and, indeed, cosmic events; hence the number 'seven thousand' is not literal, but symbolical. The fact that those who were not killed in this outbreak of judgment 'gave glory to God', does not mean that they were converted, any more than God's 'servants', Cyrus (Is. 44:28; 45:1) and Nebuchadnezzar (Jer. 25:9; 27:6; 43:10) were converted when they fulfilled God's will; see also Daniel 2:47; 3:28; 4:1ff., 34, 37. The meaning is that they acknowledged Him. And many do so when His power and glory pass before them; they are 'impressed', but their souls are not saved. It takes more than an 'impression' to cause men to bow before God in contrition and cry for mercy.

[14]*The second woe has passed; behold, the third woe is soon to come.* Now comes the final judgment!

[15]*Then the seventh angel blew his trumpet, and there were loud voices in heaven, saying, 'The kingdom of the world has become the kingdom of our Lord and of his Christ, and he shall reign for ever and ever.'* Notice that the final judgment is not described, but announced in terms of the total victory of God and Christ. The statement of verse 15 is well known as belonging to the text of Handel's 'Hallelujah Chorus'. Its embrace is vast, including the recovery of man's dominion of the universe from its discredited, satanic overlord; see Genesis 3:15; Isaiah 14:12–19; Ezekiel 28:12–19; Matthew 12:29; Luke 4.5–7; John 12:31; 14:30; 16:11; Ephesians 2:2. This is what the risen Christ declared in Matthew 28:18–20: 'All authority in heaven and on earth has been given to me. Go therefore and make disciples of all nations, baptizing them in the name of the Father and of the Son and of the Holy Spirit, teaching them to observe all that I have commanded you...'. It is declared by Christ at the beginning of the historical process of gathering in the fruits of His victory; whereas the statement in verse 15 declares the accomplishment of the task at the climactic end, when Christ has returned in power and glory to take His kingdom and reign; see 1 Corinthians 15:25.

[16]*And the twenty-four elders who sit on their thrones before God fell on their faces and worshipped God,* The twenty-four

elders reappear, as in chapters 4:4, 10; 5:5, 8, 11, 13. They are all-important since the victory of Christ over the kingdom of evil is gained not for God and for Christ as deity, as if they needed it, but for man, as the object of the divine strategy of creation and redemption. The elders sit on thrones, but the seventh trumpet blows its note of summons to all creatures to attend the consummating moment, they cannot remain on their thrones, but cast themselves down. The fact that they sit on thrones, yet ever seek to cast themselves before God, indicate that although they accept their co-reign with Christ (2 Tim. 2:12; Rev. 5:10; 20:6; 22:5), they gladly acknowledge that they are in that royal position solely and for ever by the virtues of Christ and by the mercy and grace of God. The twenty-four elders represent the church of Old and New Testament saints, making their response to the final accomplishment of the great plan of redemption. This is entirely a response of thanksgiving to God, who through Christ and His faithful church has wrought it all to His eternal glory.

[17]*saying, 'We give thanks to thee, Lord God Almighty, who art and who wast,* not 'who art to come', for He has come! *that thou hast taken thy great power and begun to reign.'* It is clear that here is described the final reign of Christ with God. Significantly the plain words of its achievement are found, not only near the end of this section (chapters 8–11), but also at a point near the close of the first half of the book. Many glories of the triumphant saints are portrayed in the Revelation, but we are not for long allowed to forget that the book was written to encourage saints in a day of persecution and trial. That is why the judicial side of the truth is never far away.

Note verse 18: [18]*'The nations raged, cf* Psalm 2:1–4, *but thy wrath came, and the time for the dead to be judged* (6:9–11, 15–17), *for rewarding thy servants, the prophets and saints, and those who fear thy name, both small and great, and for destroying the destroyers,* see 1 Corinthians 3:17, *of the earth.'* God's judgments are not arbitrary, see Psalm 98:1–2 in particular. The nations raged, but God's wrath came, which was the time for the judgment of those who had hated the Lord and His people. Nothing could be more reasonable and necessary for the preservation of God's kingdom than that the destroyers should be destroyed. All destruction is then banished to its own place, and with it all sin, fear, cruelty and death.

¹⁹*Then God's temple in heaven was opened,* a special vision is granted John into heaven itself, *and the ark of his covenant was seen within his temple;* contrast 21:22; *and there were flashes of lightning, loud noises, peals of thunder, an earth-quake, and heavy hail.* This glimpse of the ark of the covenant amid such fearsome phenomena reminds us that it contained the two tables of God's law; also that the ark became God's seat of mercy when the blood of atonement was sprinkled upon it (Lev. 16:15–16). The implication is clear that those not 'covered' by that blood through the response of faith are dealt with in terms of God's inexorable and implacable law: 'The soul that sinneth, it shall die.' (Ezek. 18:4; 20 AV) Hence the 'fireworks' reminiscent of the plague of hail and thunder (Exod. 9.22–35), and of the awful experience of Sinai (Exod. 19:16–25; 20:18–21). Concerning the ark, see 2 Samuel 6:7; 2 Chronicles 35:3; Jeremiah 3:15–18a; Hebrews 9:1, 4, 19, 20.

CHAPTER TWELVE

The Victory of Christ and his Church

12:1–17

Chapter 12 not only commences the next section of the book re-traversing the ground covered from the first to the second coming of Christ, but is the beginning of the second half of the book of Revelation. Whereas chapters 1–11 have shown the conflict between good and evil from the earthly point of view, that is, involving the church and the world, we now go on to see the conflict behind it, between Christ and the devil. Not that this ultimate conflict has been entirely hidden (*cf* the portrayal of demon forces in chapter 9), but the veil is now lifted, and, as in Job chapters 1 and 2, we see the 'high command' of both good and evil: see Isaiah 24:21–33; Luke 10:18. Further, chapter 12 stands by itself in providing both a sweep of history and a summation of the meaning of history not equalled in the Scriptures. The nearest to it is Ezekiel chapter 16 (but see Genesis 37:9), which covers in parabolic fashion the greater part of Old Testament history and the romantic and heroic story of Israel. Do not be misled by the simplicity and brevity of the narrative here: it takes huge strides in its first seven verses.

¹*and a great portent appeared in heaven, a woman clothed with the sun, with the moon under her feet, and on her head a crown of twelve stars; *²*she was with child.* The last four words hint that we are dealing with the 'maternity' of the Christ-child; and the mother (although from Genesis 3, especially verse 15, she may be characterised as Eve), is Israel, viewed as the Old Testament church, see Isaiah 50:1;

54:1; Hosea 2:1–2; Ephesians 5:32. But she is a 'mother' not only of earthly but of cosmic significance, as indeed the Almighty, speaking to Abram, used the figure of the stars in the sky (Gen. 15:5; 22:17; 26:4; Deut. 1:10; Exod. 32:13), as well as the sand on the seashore (Gen. 13:16 ['dust]; 22:17; 32:12), to describe the number of sons that his seed (descendants) would have. The universe was created as the stage for this drama: these luminaries, described as the woman's 'clothing', are but the 'lightning' of the stage. (Note the twelve stars for twelve tribes.)

...and she cried out in her pangs of birth, in anguish for delivery. Curiously enough, as Israel's plight worsened, her prophets, although fiercely realistic, became increasingly hopeful in the long view, albeit prophetic inspiration dried up. Pharisaic and apocalyptic movements in the second and first centuries BC gained impetus, presumably from the revival of the Word of God which came from the synagogues, themselves begun in captivity. The complete history of Israel during her first millennium BC is therefore paradoxically but truly portrayed as a woman crying out in birth pangs for delivery. This distress was envisaged long before the monarchy (Deut. 4:25–31; chs. 28 and 29) as well as after its decline (Is. 66:7–9; Mic. 4:10; 5:2, 3).

³*And another portent appeared in heaven; behold, a great red dragon, with seven heads and ten horns, and seven diadems upon his heads.* Note that 'heaven' here is the world of good and evil spirits in conflict (Eph. 6:12; Rev. 12:7), not God's throne. There are various figures for the evil one, or his chief servants, in the Old Testament, such as Rahab in Job 26:12–13; Isaiah 51:9; Behemoth in Job 40:15; and Leviathan in Job 41:1; Psalm 74:13–14; Isaiah 27:1. The seven heads and seven diadems suggest Satan's God-given authority as chief angel (*cf* Is. 14:12) before he fell; see Luke 4:5–7; John 12:31; 14:30; 16:11. The ten horns, Hendriksen suggests, stand for destructive power.

⁴*His tail swept down a third of the stars of heaven;* these are doubtless angels, and may refer to such as may have demonized the Cainite men in Genesis 6.1–4 (Delitzsch), see also Job 38:7; Daniel 8:10–11; 1 Peter 3:19–20; 2 Peter 2;4; Jude 6; and the first book of Enoch; *and cast them to the*

*earth. And the dragon stood before the woman who was
about to bear a child, that he might devour her child when
she brought it forth*; The dragon standing before the woman
towards the time of her delivery expresses with marvellous
succinctness the persistent, single-minded determination of
Satan throughout the Old Testament ages to destroy the
Christ-child as soon as He is born—not having succeeded in
destroying the woman (Israel) beforehand. Read the succession of Joseph's dreams, in Matthew chapters 1 and 2, to see
the Child's danger then.

*⁵she brought forth a male child, one who is to rule all the
nations with a rod of iron*, note the firmness: this power is
also given to the saints who conquer (Rev. 2.26, 27), *but her
child was caught up to God and to his throne*, the Incarnation
is completely telescoped, with no summary of it, even as in
John 20;30–31, or in the Apostles' Creed: 'born...
suffered...crucified...descended...rose again...ascended',
because the emphasis is on the Church left on earth to
survive, *⁶and the woman fled into the wilderness, where she
has a place prepared by God, in which to be nourished for one
thousand two hundred and sixty days*. Note the paradox of a
'wilderness...prepared by God'. This speaks of the divine
care for the Lord's own (John 10:27–29) after Satan's
unsuccessful attempt to destroy the Christ-child. We see
hints of that care in 11:3–6 and 12:14, and recall the
element in the Elijah story relevant here, his nourishment
in the wilderness (1 Kings 17:4). Christian history abounds
in instances of God's wonderful preservation and survival of
the Jewish people, despite all their trials (*cf* their estab-
lishment of the State of Israel in 1948 after the Hitlerian
massacres!) and the preservation and survival of the Christian Church under brutal suppressions, including contemporary instances in Russia and China.

Note that the woman is the same after the Child as before,
since she represents the one people of God, Old Testament
and New Testament. She is left on earth in a hostile world,
but with the promise, 'I am with you always unto the end of
the age' (Matt. 28:20).

⁷Now war arose in heaven, This is not Christ's actual
historical victory on the cross, but the resultant victorious

conflict of the church in the heavenlies, governed, directed and controlled by the prayers and witness of the saints on earth from Christ's High Priestly place by His Father in heaven. The victory of Christ in history is the focal point of the eternal victory ('the Lamb slain from the foundation of the world', 13:8), which enabled Daniel, for example (chapter 10), to triumph in the heavenlies over a malign spirit and demon prince hundreds of years before Christ actually died. The effects of that divine event, wrought in the midst of history, are therefore retrospective, as well as prospective. The war in heaven has its epicentre on earth: it is not the heavenly (in the sense of the angelic) which affects the earthly, but the earthly (the church) which affects the heavenly (Eph 6:12. This is the crux of Christ's work for us. When it is understood, the remainder of the passage (7–12) is seen as describing the victories of the saints over Satan and his kingdom throughout the ages; see verse 11.

*Michael and his angels fighting against the dragon; and the dragon and his angels fought, *[8]*but they were defeated and there was no longer any place for them in heaven.* Note that the results of this defeat, from Satan's point of view, are not described until verse 12, when he is angry 'because he knows that his time is short', and comes down to the place where heavenly battles are decided, namely the earth.

Observe also that Michael is the archangel with special responsibility for Israel (see Dan. 10:13, 21; 12:1; Jude 9), as, presumably, he has special responsibility also for the New Testament Israel, the Church. He is now able to tackle the great dragon himself, as a result of Christ's defeat of him. This is wonderful news. Satan is no longer to be feared, albeit he is to be respected ('know your enemy'), since he has still power where Christ's victory is not invoked by faith; but where that victory's power is invoked, we have authority over him, and it is this authority of faith which affords the holy angels freedom to act. (Note their dependence upon the saints!) For this startling truth, see Daniel 10, and Ephesians 6:11–12.

⁹*And the great dragon was thrown down,* see Luke 10:18; John 12:31, *that ancient serpent, who is called the Devil,* Diabolos = Slanderer, *and Satan* (Adversary), who, Morris says from Job 1:6 and Zechariah 3:11 came to be known as the accuser of men before God, *the deceiver of the world—he was thrown down to the earth, and his angels were thrown down with him.*

¹⁰*And I,* John, *heard a loud voice in heaven,* whose is the voice? angel's or man's? *saying, 'Now the salvation and the power and the kingdom of our God and the authority of his Christ have come, for the accuser of our brethren has been thrown down, who accuses them day and night,* without interruption, *before our God.'* Satan still accuses, perhaps even more plausibly now since he knows our power. Yet, as Christians, if we know the truth that all his accusations are invalidated by Christ's sacrifice on our behalf (see Rom. 8:31–34; Zech. 3:1–5; and 1 Enoch 40:7), we shall be able to resist him, 'and,' promises James 4:7; 1 Peter 5:8–9, 'he will flee.'

²²'*And they have conquered him by the blood of the Lamb,* this is the saints' own victory over Satan and all his powers, on the ground of Christ's once-for-all victorious death: the fact cannot be too categorically and emphatically stated, *and by the word of their testimony*; The mode of the saints' victory over the powers of evil is their stand upon the word of their testimony to the all-powerful fact of Christ's death. 'We preach Christ cruficied,' wrote Paul to the Corinthians, 'a stumbling block to Jews and folly to Gentiles, but to those who are called, both Jews and Gentiles, Christ the power of God and wisdom of God.' (But see the whole passage from 1 Corinthians 1:17 to 2:5, where we read of the resounding effect of the Apostle's testimony to the power of Christ's death.) *for they loved not their lives even unto death.'* We see how far saints may go in testifying to the death of Christ and its power. It is the spirit of Jesus Himself (see John 12:25; Luke 14:27); the spirit of Paul also (see Phil. 1:21; Col. 1:24); and of all who share the potency of Christ's death and resurrection when they work out in their lives what the Spirit has wrought into them (Phil 2:12–13).

¹²'*Rejoice then, O heaven and you that dwell therein!'* In

view of the victory in the heavenly places recorded in Daniel chapter 10, it is important to understand that the power of Michael the archangel over the demonic prince of the king of Greece, gained through Daniel's three weeks of prayer, flowed from the once-for-all victorious death of Christ as an eternal fact (see Rev. 5:6; 13:8) *before* it took place historically, no less than the victories of the saints after it. If this seems incomprehensible, it needs to be remembered that the salvation of the Old Testament saints by faith (recorded in Heb. 11) was procured no less by the death of Christ than our salvation now, their sins admittedly being 'passed over' (Rom. 3:25) until that death was objectively accomplished in history. This does not reduce the importance of the historical act, but increases it, and shows both its necessity and the eternal range of its efficacy. In this connection, although Revelation chapter 12 is in some ways more sequential than other chapters and passages, we are not to read it as a chronological record of events, but as a series of dynamic pictures and images of events wrought out in history, but possessing eternal significance.

'But woe to you, O earth and sea, for the devil has come down to you in great wrath.' Following the work of Christ, the devil has a new awareness that the point of conflict between him and Christ is now on earth, in the lives, witness and warfare of the saints, who are authorised and empowered to wage war upon hostile angelic forces in heaven by the exercise of faith in Christ's victory. If we say that this is what Daniel did in chapter 10, we must also say that, since Christ's work, the power is now authenticated by Christ's session at the right hand of the Father, and is offered to the Gentiles universally (Eph. 3:1–6), as formerly, strictly speaking, it was offered only to and through the Jews.

'because he knows that his time is short!' Not only is the devil's sphere of activity now much more on earth, but his rage increases as he sees his end approaching. His desire, naturally, is to do as much harm as possible to Christ and His cause while he can. This he does by seeking to hurt Christ's church. We must never forget this. The following verses describe the lines Satan's 'great wrath' takes: [13]*And*

*when the dragon saw that he had been thrown down to the
earth, he pursued the woman who had borne the male child.*
[14]*But the woman was given the two wings of the great eagle
that she might fly from the serpent into the wilderness, to the
place where she is to be nourished for a time, and times, and
half a time.*

The figure of eagles' wings is biblical, see Exodus 19:4;
Deuteronomy 32:11; Isaiah 40:28–31. It speaks of the
powerful support the Lord gives to His persecuted church to
fly from the evil one into the sheltered place where she is to
be nourished during the gospel era (see v.6). This thought is
beautifully expressed in the Shepherd Psalm, 23:5. The
enemy prowls around, seeking to alarm and distract the
saints, but he cannot harm God's own (1 Pet. 3:13) if they
ward him off by faith, and refuse to be terrified by him. The
whole paradox and tension created by living the Christian
life (that is, the heavenly life, on earth) are summed up in
verse 14 and in Psalm 23:5—we are being nourished in a
wilderness where danger always threatens, but harm never
comes. It is the tension of being poised, in fact, between
heaven and hell, yet utterly safe, which makes our growth
in faith a wonderful possibility. For, 'Satan trembles when
he sees, the weakest saint upon his knees' (William Cowper).

There is, therefore, a double incentive to draw near to
Christ, learn of Him, and know Him. On the one hand, we
have the dangers of the wilderness; on the other, the delights
of His table in the wilderness (Ps. 78:19). The picture of the
Lord preparing a table for His own, and graciously anointing
their heads with oil in the presence of their enemies is
calculated to bring assurance to the most fearful soul

[15]*The serpent poured water like a river out of his mouth
after the woman, to sweep her away with the flood.* [16]*But the
earth came to the help of the woman, and the earth opened its
mouth and swallowed the river which the dragon had poured
from his mouth.* The scene is exceedingly dramatic. See
Exodus 15:12; Numbers 16 (the story of Korah); and Isaiah
43:1–2. Hendriksen suggests that the rivers may be a
'stream of lies, delusions, religious -isms', philosophical
falsehoods, political utopias, quasi-scientic dogma…but the
true church is not fooled.' (*More than Conquerors,* p.172).

The general explanation is surely that nature, despite its fallenness, is God's nature and, groaning as it is for deliverance from its unsought fruitlessness (Rom. 8:20–22), is on the side of God's children, and helps them.

What is meant by the earth opening its mouth to swallow the engulfing waters? The commentators are not much help. 'As regards the original meaning of this verse we are wholly in the dark.' (Charles, *The International Critical Commentary,* p.331)! Perhaps there is no better explanation than that death and the grave are so often the solution to human hostility against Christ's church. There is no need, fortunately, to ask God to deal drastically with the church's enemies; for while we are on earth we may never be sufficiently objective to do so without the danger of vindictiveness (but see Rev. 6:9–11). God sees when His saints have had enough, and in kindness removes the human cause of their affliction. We do not need to be vengeful, although we may see God act in his divinely perfect justice from time to time.

[17]*Then the dragon was angry with the woman,* The causes of Satan's anger naturally multiply as his subtlest stratagems go awry, and the various departments of his plundered empire progressively favour his Enemy! We are well warned to watch for his fury (1 Pet. 5:8). *and went off to make war on the rest of her offspring, on those who keep the commandments of God and bear testimony to Jesus.* The latter clause defines the former: the 'rest of her offspring' are those who remain true to God and to His Son by their lives and witness. But we are left in no doubt as to the persecutions we shall suffer if we abide true to God and His Son; see Acts 14:22; Romans 8:17, 35–37; 2 Timothy 2:12, 3:10–13; 2 Peter 3:8–17.

And he stood on the sand of the sea. Another reading, 'I stood,' would refer to John, but there is little doubt that it is Satan. He stands between land and sea. Three powers, under Satan, appear in the course of this section: the beasts from the sea (13:1), and from the land (13:11), and Babylon (14:8). The beast from the sea represents nations and governments, the beast from the land, false religions and philosophies, whereas Babylon the city represents worldly seduction. Satan commands all three as, respectively, his hand, mind, and wiles; and he works through them to conceal himself. See 1 John 2:18; 2 Thessalonians 2:3–12. We should remember that the 'last days' began with the completion of Christ's redeeming and victorious work, and that we are drawing nearer to the 'last hour', when many antichrists (1 John 2:18) will give place to the final antichrist.

CHAPTER THIRTEEN

The Beasts
13:1–18

¹*And I saw a beast rising out of the sea,* compare 'and the sea was no more' (21:1) as representing wordly government and power, *with ten horns and seven heads, with ten diadems upon its horns,* and contrast 12:3, for the seven heads doubtless represent seven empires, spanning history. The diadems are crowns of authority, not wreaths *(stephanos)* of victory; *and a blasphemous name upon its heads.* That name should be reserved for the Almighty Himself, because it expresses His divine authority.

²*And the beast that I saw was like a leapord* (panther), *its feet were like a bear's, and its mouth was like a lion's mouth.* The three elements of this beast are taken from Daniel 7:4–6. The fourth beast of Daniel 7:7 may not appear here because of its indescribable hideousness. This beast is an amalgam of three of Daniel's beasts. According to Daniel 2 they represent in reverse order, Babylon (head of gold, the lion?); Medo-Persia (breast and arms of silver, the bear?); Greece (belly and thighs of bronze, the leopard?). The most important thing is not to identify the various elements with particular empires, but to see that the beast in composite fashion represents the essentials of wordly rule and authority. As the text is about to say, the beast owes its power and authority, whatever the time and place, to the dragon himself. *And to it the dragon gave his power and his throne and great authority.* That is to say, it is the devil who rules the ungodly world. All its powers, whatever men think,

are under his authority and in his power.

[3]*One of its heads seemed to have a mortal wound, but its mortal wound was healed, and the whole earth followed the beast with wonder.* If the seven heads represent seven world empires throughout history, which one had a mortal wound and was healed? Most people think it was Rome, with Nero as the mortally wounded head, since it was believed by some that he was too evil to remain dead and would revive again! 'Others think that Caligula is meant, for he had a dangerous illness and recovered.' (Morris, p.167). Certainly in the time of the apostle John, Rome was in its heyday, as the New Testament makes plain, and she certainly had a succession of emperors, such as Julius Caesar, Augustus, Claudius, Vespasian and Titus who were declared to be divine at their death and accepted as such by the people—the deadly wound healed. But to localise the description is not to confine it to ancient history, for evil elements in men and dynasties recur. Satan sees to that (2 Thess 2:9–10).

[4]*Men worshipped the dragon, for he had given his authority to the beast, and they worshipped the beast, saying, 'Who is like the beast, and who can fight against it?'* It may seem harder in materialistic ages to believe in a religion which worships the devil, but ours makes it more than credible, since there is an air of worship about so many of the pursuits which enamour and glamourise—sport, entertainment, and political and military power among them. Little do men realise that the element which draws their wonder is the hidden presence and action of evil beings. Note also the tendency to materialise the object of worship from the legendary dragon to the actual beast. That is why verse 4 ends with a religious challenge, and godly counterparts of it may be seen in the literature of Israel, *eg* Exodus 15:11; Psalm 35:10.

[5]*And the beast was given,* note the delegated authority, *a mouth uttering haughty and blasphemous words, and it was allowed to exercise authority for forty-two months;* The interpretation adopted, namely that what follows goes on for the duration of the time between the two comings of Christ (forty-two months), presents a grim prospect for the church in the future. There is no doubt that the church

D

throughout gospel ages has suffered as described, but however generally we may want to take the prophecy, it is clear that it has a cumulative effect, and that the situation of the church will get worse towards the day of Christ's second coming.

Another view of the later stages of the day of grace may be taken (and has been taken by Iain Murray in his book, *The Puritan Hope*) from Romans chapters 9—11, and it is the present writer's opinion that these two views need to be held together. This is not as difficult as may appear, since it is the common experience of the church throughout the ages that when she is spiritually in the ascendant the enemy of souls is most active. This intensifies the conflict and creates the seeming paradox which drives Bible scholars to take sides between a day of revival and a day of disaster for the church towards the end of the age. Can the two extremes be simultaneous? There is certainly no doubt from Revelation chapter 20 that there will be a major recrudescence of evil near the end; but the extremes need to be seen as reacting upon each other.

⁶*it opened its mouth to utter blasphemies against God, blaspheming his name and his dwelling, that is, those who dwell in heaven.* The blasphemies against God are in respect of the church, either the church already triumphant, see Revelation 6:9–11; or the church on earth whose citizenship is already in heaven (Phil. 3:20); yet God tabernacling with her (the word 'dwelling' is tent) see Revelation 21:2–4).

⁷*Also it was allowed to make war on the saints and to conquer them.* Here is stated the truth about the position of the church in relation to evil during the gospel age, as Ephesians 6:12–13, with its continuous present tense, shows: 'For we wrestle…against rulers, authorities, against the world (*cosmos*) rulers of this darkness, against spiritual hosts of evil in the heavenlies. Therefore take the whole armour of God, that ye may be able to withstand the evil day…', Any failure to take these words seriously must mislead the church as to the true state of affairs between God and the devil in the meantime, and between the church and the world. *And authority was given it over every tribe and people and tongue and nation,* This clearly predicts a

universal overspread of evil as the devil's answer and counterpart to the promise of Christ since before the end of the age that 'this gospel of the kingdom will be preached throughout the whole world, as a testimony to all nations, and then the end will come.' (Matt. 24:14).

⁸*and all who dwell on earth will worship it, every one whose name has not been written before the foundation of the world in the book of life of the Lamb that was slain. See 2* Thessalonians 2:4: Morris points out that the words 'those who dwell on the earth' recur in the Revelation a number of times, *eg* 6:10; 8:13; 11:10; 13:8,14; 14:6; 17:8; with a similar phrase twice more: 13:12; 17:2. These always seem to refer to 'unregenerate mankind as a whole' (Morris, p.109), the unregenerate being described negatively in terms of those not destined to salvation. Those who are, are 'chosen in him (Christ) before the foundation of the world' (Eph. 1:4). See also Matthew 25:34; 2 Thessalonians 2:13; 1 Peter 1:19–20; Revelation 17:8. Note the close connection between their election and the death of Christ: His is 'the book of life of the Lamb that was slain'. The statement implies that only those who are secure by the eternal election of God will be safe in the day of great tribulation. God will keep them. That this is an unequivocal and categorical statement of momentous and abiding validity is made plain by verse 9.

⁹*If any one has an ear, let him hear:* That eternal security does not necessarily absolve from physical suffering is made plain by the first half of verse 10: ¹⁰*If any one is to be taken captive, to captivity he goes;* see Jeremiah 15:2; 43:11; *if anyone slays with the sword, with the sword must he be slain.* There are two readings concerning the sword, passive or, as in RSV, active. 'If anyone slays' seems to be out of accord with the tenor of the passage, and with its origin in Jeremiah 15:2, as with the final statement of the verse. See NIV *Here is a call for the endurance and faith of the saints.* It is a call not unheeded by those destined for heaven, since electing grace supplies the faith by which persecution and even death for Christ's sake are faced. Hence the command in Revelation 2:10. See also Job 13:15, AV: (KJV) 'Though he slay me, yet will I trust in him.' Justice will triumph; see Revelation 6:10–11.

[11]*Then I saw another beast which rose out of the earth; it had two horns like a lamb and it spoke like a dragon.* This beast is the diabolical counterpart of the Lion and the Lamb, see Revelation 5:5–6. He is the false prophet (16:13; 19:20), and represents false religion and false philosophy in innumerable forms throughout the entire dispensation; see 2 Corinthians 11:14. [12]*It exercises all the authority of the first beast in its presence, and makes the earth and its inhabitants worship the first beast, whose mortal wound was healed.* The second beast, the false prophet, is clearly in the power of the first beast, who in turn is under the authority of the dragon, Satan. It ought not to surprise us that religion can be used so easily by ungodly power (see comments on verse 4), since worldly power (the first beast) is itself under the power of the dragon, whose whole aim is to draw away the worship of men from God and Christ to himself. This explains the religious influences brought to bear upon the German people to embrace Nazism, which Niemoller and Bonhoeffer bravely resisted. These influences have also been strong in communist Russia and China. Note that although the second beast represents religion and philosophy, it emerges from the earth: see earthly wisdom in 1 Corinthians, chs. 1, 2; James 3:15; and in Philippians 3:19.

[13]*It works great signs, even making fire come down from heaven to earth in the sight of men;* see Mark 13:22; 2 Thessalonians 2:9: note that this is what the prophets of Baal could not do in the presence of Elijah (1 Kings 18:29): Pharaoh's magicians also were limited (Exod. 8:7, 18, 19; 9:11); but this is the day of Satan's power (*cf.* Lk. 22:53), especially towards the end of the gospel age: [14]*and by the signs which it is allowed to work in the presence of the beast, it deceives those who dwell on earth,* the unregenerate, *bidding them make an image for the beast which was wounded by the sword and yet lived;* the implication is that not only Christ may have His life restored, but evil also, although it imitates in order to deceive, because it has no original power; see 2 Thessalonians, 2:9. [15]*and it was allowed to give breath to the image of the beast so that the image of the beast should even speak,* Nebuchadnezzar's image did not speak (Dan. 3), *and to cause those who would not worship the*

image of the beast to be slain. Note 'it was allowed': beyond the triumvirate of evil stands the Almighty, in perfect control of all things. It has always been the intention of the spirit of Islam to gain power—and to seek to maintain it where it was endangered—by the sword: the methods it uses may be more subtly refined today, but Arab Christians may still be 'liquidated' for their faith in Christ. The modern religion of Communism is hardly less ruthless, although vastly more cunning.

[16]*Also it causes all, both small and great, both rich and poor, both free and slave, to be marked on the right hand or the forehead,* [17]*so that no one can buy or sell unless he has the mark, that is, the name of the beast or the number of its name.* The tyrranical and ruthless limitations of freedom in our day make this far from improbable.

[18]*This calls for wisdom: let him who has understanding reckon the number of the beast, for it is a human number, its number is six hundred and sixty-six.* Note, first, that wisdom, not mere knowledge, is called for in understanding this mystery. It may be remarked that in this century we have seen new manifestations of totalitarian government which the Victorian era of the nineteenth century would scarcely have believed possible.

As to the number of the beast, which is a human number, many ingenious suggestions have been made concerning it throughout Christian history. In the ancient world the letters of the alphabet were used for numbers. Various names in Latin, Greek and Hebrew have thus been applied to the problem, with no satisfactory solution, but rather producing ludicrous attempts to make selected names fit. Doubtless the most satisfactory attempt to understand the three-fold number six is to say that, since the number seven in Scripture is undoubtedly the perfect number, the number six may be regarded as the number of man, who by his imperfections and inadequacies does not attain the perfect number seven. One of the chief values of this view is its simplicity. The question maybe asked: Why three sixes? Do they represent six hundred and sixty-six, or do they represent three distinct but related numerical entities? A plausible answer may be that if they do not represent six hundred and sixty-six, but three distinct entities, they may represent the triumvirate of evil, the dragon, and the two beasts. Certainly these three in their evil plans are chiefly concerned with man. For further discussion on this point, see Hendriksen, Morris and Charles.

CHAPTER FOURTEEN

The Song of the Redeemed, and the Mark of the Beast

14:1–20

We now come to the final chapter of the section, chapters 12–14, and to the climax, towards the end of the age, in respect of both the saints and the wicked. *Then I looked, and lo, on Mount Zion stood the Lamb*, see Joel 2:32 for the summing up of the 'pentecostal' passage quoted in Acts chapter 2. This concerns the gathering of all who seek the Lord and call on His name in order that they may be 'delivered' to Mount Zion and Jerusalem, undoubtedly heavenly Jerusalem, see Psalm 125:1 and Hebrews 12:22. The event of Pentecost is a precursor of the heavenly state just as Jesus' transfiguration was a preview of His glory to come. *and with him a hundred and forty-thousand who had his name and his Father's name written on their foreheads.* These, summed up under the representative number, one hundred and forty-four thousand, are the sealed saints in heaven, as we saw them sealed in chapter 7:2–4. The seal with the names of the Lamb and the Father is counterfeited in the 'mark of the beast'; see 13:16–17.

²And I heard a voice from heaven like the sound of many waters and like the sound of loud thunder; the voice I heard was like the sound of harpers on their harps, ³and they sing a new song before the throne and before the four living creatures and before the elders. No one could learn that song except the hundred and forty-four thousand who had been redeemed from the earth. No comment is required here, except to encourage all who read to seek divine inspiration

in order to enter into the beauty, wonder and glory of the
scene. The beauty is moral, and springs from the saints'
perfect allegiance to the Crucified. Note that the experience
(in modern parlance) is not only 'video' but 'audio'; the sound
being not only overwhelmingly powerful, but inexpressibly
beautiful.

⁴*It is these who have not defiled themselves with women, for
they are chaste;* or, virgins, see 2 Corinthians 11:2. It ought
to be clear that no disparagement of holy matrimony is
intended (see *eg* 1 Cor. 6:15–20; Eph. 5:21–33). But since
human marriage is itself an analogy of the divine union of
Christ with His pure bride, the church, that analogy is here
employed to portray the original and ultimate reality itself,
the union of the church with Christ; see Matthew 22:30.
Soldiers in ancient Israel were warned against defilement
with pagan women during campaign, see the holy war in
Deuteronomy ch.20; Deuteronomy 23:9–10; 1 Samuel 21:5;
2 Samuel 11:11. Here, the 144,000 are soldiers of the Lamb!
it is these who follow the Lamb wherever he goes; union with
Christ implies complete identity and the closest association
with Him in all things, for the reason about to be stated;
these have been redeemed from mankind, 'Redeemed'
(purchased) 'from mankind' is a striking phrase, under-
lining their specific election in relation to the atonement,
see 1 Corinthians 6:20; 7:23; Revelation 5:9. This statement
emphasises that the Lord's chosen are taken from among
men, and are therefore no longer to be regarded as belonging to the world, see John 15:18–19; 17:9, 14, 16; 18:36; 1
John 2:15; 3:13; Philippians 3:20–21. *as first fruits for God
and the Lamb,* Christ is the first fruits of his own resurrection (1 Cor. 15:23) and the church is the first fruits of the
redemption of the universe (Jas. 1:18; Rom. 8:19–23), *and
in their mouth no lie was found, for they are spotless.* See
Isaiah 53:9c; Zephaniah 3:13; Hebrews 6:18; 1 John 2:21;
Colossians 3:9; Romans 9:1; 2 Corinthians 11:31; Galatians
1:20; 1 Timothy 2:7; Revelation 21:27. They take their
character from their Christ-born disposition, and are
utterly true to it. The unqualified truth of their character
and their spotlessness arises from the fact that they are in
heaven, and are therefore delivered from the body of their

humiliation (Phil. 3:21).

⁶*Then I saw another angel flying in midheaven, with an eternal gospel to proclaim to those who dwell on earth, to every nation and tribe and tongue and people;* ⁷*and he said with a loud voice, 'Fear God and give him glory, for the hour of his judgment has come; and worship him who made heaven and earth, the sea and the fountains of water.'* Clearly this is towards the end of the age, when the final invitation and gospel offer—here called the 'eternal gospel' for obvious reasons—is made. The gospel is stated, not in redemptive terms, but in terms of final warning, which concern Who God is, the worship which all His creatures owe Him, and the fact that the great judgment in respect of these things is at hand.

⁸*Another angel, a second, followed, saying, 'Fallen, fallen is Babylon the great, she who made all nations drink the wine of her impure passion.'* This second angel takes the final events of the gospel age a stage further, by announcing the destruction of the spirit of Babylon, the spirit of the first beast, with its worldly pride and power derived from the dragon. Here we see the Almighty dealing with the root cause of the sins of men and nations, 'her impure passion'. See Psalm 75:7–8; Jeremiah 25:15–17.

⁹*And another angel, a third, followed them, saying with a loud voice, 'If any one worships the beast and its image,* note how the singular 'any one' emphasises the free choice of the individual, *and receives a mark on his forehead or on his hand,* note the character of the fraud which marks the beast worshippers (see Rev. 17:5); it is the Babel spirit, which goes back to Genesis 11, and affects both head and hand, thought and action; ¹⁰*he also shall drink the wine of God's wrath, poured unmixed,* all the restraint of the infinitely patient and long-suffering Lord of the universe is now taken away, see 2 Thessalonians 2:7, *into the cup of his anger,* It is exceedingly foolish to identify or associate the wrath of God and of the Lamb (6:16–17; 11:18) with the fitful passions of men. The wrath of God is his settled disposition of implacable opposition to sin and evil. His judgment is all the more sure because of his former restraint. *and he shall be tormented with fire and brimstone,* the eternal fire of God's

wrath is described in extreme physical terms, not merely to shock and horrify, but also to indicate that the spiritual reality will be far worse than any earthly fire; *in the presence of the holy angels and in the presence of the Lamb.*'

We may observe that a psychological or emotional approach to these words might easily prove intolerably embarrassing. But the nearer we travel into the heart of the Eternal, learning that He is 'wonderfully kind', the more we see how utterly justified He is in dealing faithfully with those who finally spurn His grace. The eternal activity of the wrath of God, therefore, is not such as some think the Almighty ought to be ashamed of, nor such as He ought to perpetrate in a corner; but is altogether right and just, and therefore to be approved, although, like Him, we need take no pleasure in the death of the wicked. Indeed, we must seek to think on the subject from the heavenly standpoint, namely, that the eternal God in His redemptive work is dealing with fallen sinners who, apart from grace, are, without exception, deserving of wrath and punishment, else our human sensitivity to the eternal punishment of the wicked will lead us astray.

In this connection it may be helpful to meditate on the *motive* of such punishment as described by our Lord Himself in Matthew 25. The wicked who are to 'go away into eternal punishment' are those who have entirely lacked compassion for their fellows, since they had no love for Christ. Those who are incapable of feeling the love of Christ cannot, of course, return it, either to Him or to his needy ones. There is therefore no alternative open to them but banishment from God, which experience, even at its most negative, is bound to involve positive suffering. It is perhaps also fair to say that although the rich man in Luke 16 was in torment, and longed for Lazarus to come and ease his pain, there is no scriptural sign that he wanted to pass from his side to the other. Would the other side have been a worse 'hell' to him?

[11]'*And the smoke of their torment goes up for ever and ever; and they have no rest, day or night, these worshippers of the beast and its image, and whoever receives the mark of its name.*' This exceedingly terrifying statement is not given to harrow feelings, but as a warning to show the connection

between the wordly god which men worship and the state of heart and mind to which they ultimately arrive, a state not temporal but eternal. This is the opposite of the satisfying abandon of the worshippers of the Lord in 5:12–14, and of the experience of the glorified saints in 7:15–17: the restlessness of evil is a frequent theme of Scripture, eg Job 1:7; 2:2; Isaiah 57:20–21; Matthew 12:43–45; 1 Peter 5:8.

[12]*Here is a call for the endurance of the saints, those who keep the commandments of God and the faith of Jesus.* The focus moves from the wicked to the blessed, with a call to the saints to endure. Their sufferings, however dreadful and alarming in prospect, are but temporal, whereas the sufferings of those who yield or succumb to God's enemies are for ever. Beyond the quality of life chosen, there is the end to be achieved, and this is a prime consideration for all whose prospects are not foreshortened by spiritual blindness. None the less, endurance here is not, and could never be, a mere holding on to another way of life to escape hell. It derives its inspiration from the nature of the life in which it participates, one of obedience and faith on the basis of love. No mere fear of hell can ever save, although it may drive men into the arms of God, and thus constrain them to taste His love. That is why the word 'Blessed', about to be uttered from heaven, is addressed to integrated souls who have lived their lives consistently, albeit not perfectly. In heaven men will simply enjoy the fruit of the life they have lived on earth. They endured, not with a view to mere reward, but in present enjoyment of God, whatever the cost.

[13]*And I heard a voice from heaven saying, 'Write this: Blessed are the dead who die in the Lord henceforth.' 'Blessed indeed,' says the Spirit, 'that they may rest from their labours, for their deeds follow them!'* This is the second of seven occurrences of the word 'Blessed' (see 1:3). There is difficulty with 'henceforth', whether it goes with what proceeds, or what follows. What definition of time is made here? The answer is that the present announcement is penultimate to the final glory, when the harvest of the earth is reaped, and the longings of the disembodied saints (Rev. 6:9–11) are fulfilled, because the persecution of the saints on earth is at an end, and all the saints will now be clothed

with resurrection bodies, see 2 Corinthians 4:16—5:5. The 'henceforth' therefore defines the precise point of time as at the climax of the last things. Before Christ came and died, the Old Testament saints at death were blessed as 'just men' ('These all died in faith', Heb. 11:13), but after Christ's work they are described as 'just men made perfect'. (Heb. 12:23) Now the blessedness of those separated by death from their 'bodies of humiliation' is completed by their resurrection at the great consummation. Their rest is now perfect (contrast Rev. 6.9–11), and 'their works' of faith are honoured. The importance of deeds of faith, stressed in both verses 12 and 13 is supported by many other New Testament passages; *eg* 1 Corinthians 3.10–15; 2 Corinthians 5:10; James 2:18–25; Revelation 19:8; 22:11–12. Consider, also, the fulness of the truth concering the doctrine of rewards for faithfulness found in the New Testament.

[14]*Then I looked, and lo, a white cloud, and seated on the cloud one like a son of man, with a golden crown on his head, and a sharp sickle in his hand.* The picture at this juncture is clear: one with the *appearance* of the son of man means that a high angel (see 'another angel', v.15), representing the Son of Man, comes to reap the fruits of the earth's wickedness. This is precisely what our Lord describes in Matthew 13:37–39.

[15]*And another angel came out of the temple (sanctuary), calling with a loud voice to him who sat upon the cloud, 'Put in your sickle, and reap, for the hour to reap has come, for the harvest of the earth is fully ripe.'* Our Lord has the word for this also, in Matthew 13:30. [16]*So he who sat upon the cloud swung his sickle on the earth, and the earth was reaped.*

We come now to the vintage. [17]*And another angel came out of the temple in heaven, and he too had a sharp sickle.* [18]*Then another angel came out from the altar,* for 'altar' see 6:9; 8:3–5; *the angel who has power* (authority) *over fire, and he called with a loud voice to him who had the sharp sickle, 'Put in your sickle, and gather the clusters of the vine of the earth, for its grapes are ripe.'* These words obviously derive from Joel 3:13. Nor should the beauty of the figure, or the language, dissuade us from envisaging and accepting the grim event described, which is preparatory to the final judgment of the wicked. It is therefore a fearful image, which is fully realised only when we think of the redness of the juice of the grape trampled under foot—like blood!

[19]*So the angel swung his sickle on the earth and gathered the vintage of the earth, and threw it into the great wine press of the wrath of God;* [20]*and the wine press was trodden,* see Revelation 19:15b, *outside the city,* see Hebrews 13:12, *and blood flowed from the wine press, as high as a horse's bridle, for one thousand six hundred stadia* (about one hundred and eight-four miles). Morris says it is probably 'the product of sixteen (the square of four, the number of the earth which is the abode of the wicked), and one hundred (the square of ten, the number of completeness).' (p.186). The best commentary on this passage is Isaiah 63:1–4. Our thoughts on reading and pondering it are best left to the imagination.

CHAPTER FIFTEEN

The Song of the Lamb, and the Seven Plagues
15:1–8

Chapters 15 and 16, according to the present interpretation, comprise the fifth section of the book, but the division is not clear-cut, since the theme seems to follow on from chapter 14, although we regarded that as a climax and ending. It is only as we read on that we see the new movement, one of almost unrelieved wrath and judgment.

The section describes God's final acts of judgment upon Christ-rejectors throughout the gospel ages; 'final' because, as it turns out, they have rejected their last chance to repent. It is clear from 16:9, 11, 21 (*cf.* 9:20, 21) that men would choose hell rather than capitulate to God. This may be illustrated from Old Testament history. Israel's acts of destruction of her enemies, commanded by God, are surely in the same category; see Genesis 15:16b and, *eg* Deuteronomy 7:1–5.

¹Then I saw another portent in heaven, great and wonderful, seven angels with seven plagues, which are the last, for with them the wrath of God is ended. ²And I saw what appeared to be a sea of glass mingled with fire; we may understand the transparency of the glass mingled with fire to express the utter probity of God's judgment and, therefore, their vindication; *and those who had conquered the beast and its image and the number of its name, standing beside the sea of glass with harps of God in their hands.* So far from those who escape these horrors lamenting the destruction of the beast worshippers, the victorious saints rejoice rather at the triumph of righteousness. This is always how God's judgments must be viewed, as a necessary, almost reluctant liquidation of forces inimical to the glory of God in the interests of the blessing of the saints. God has no other purpose for judgment than His glory. He has no pleasure in the death of the wicked, but it pleases Him to remove barriers to His blessed will among the saints.

³*And they sing the song of Moses, the servant of God, and the song of the Lamb,* this brings together beautifully the two dispensations of grace, that of the law and the gospel, since they belong to each other, see Galatians 3:24; saying, '*Great and wonderful are thy deeds, O Lord God the Almighty! Just and true are thy ways, O King of the ages!* Note how the 'deeds' and the 'ways' are brought together, as in Psalm 103:7. ⁴*Who shall not fear and glorify thy name, O Lord? For thou alone art holy.* 'Holy' here must have the sense of having perfect probity. *All nations shall come and worship thee, for thy judgments,* judicial sentences, see Genesis 18:25, *have been revealed.*' Surely there is a wonderfully solemn beauty about the victorious saints rejoicing in the victory of God over those creatures on the enemy's side who have sought to foil the divine purpose. Nothing could be more seemly, chaste, and honourable. The only alternative conceivable would be to deplore God's judgments (as unbelievers suggest), but that would bring into contempt the whole basis of their own happy position, and the God who made it possible. It is too much to expect, despite the fierceness of God's judgments. Men cannot have it both ways!

⁵*After this I looked, and the temple of the tent of witness in heaven was opened,* ⁶*and out of the temple came the seven angels with the seven plagues, robed in pure bright linen,* altogether appropriate for a holy task, *and their breasts girded with golden girdles.* ⁷*And one of the four living creatures gave the seven angels seven golden bowls full of the wrath of God who lives for ever and ever;* ⁸*and the temple was filled with smoke from the glory of God and from his power, and no one could enter the temple until the seven plagues of the seven angels were ended.*

This is all utterly pure and holy, and no one can read it

worthily without being moved by the impeccable chasteness and regal purity of the picture. It is taken, of course, from the Old Testament accounts of God's visible glory entering His house while Israel was in the wilderness (Exod. 40:34); then in the Temple at Jerusalem at the dedication in Solomon's day (1 Kings 8:10, 11; 2 Chron. 7:2); in Isaiah's own personal experience at his call (Is. 6:4); and in Ezekiel's ideal vision of the Temple to come (Ezek. 10:4; 44:4). This visible glory, after the captivity, yielded (Jer. 3:16) to the conception of the Lord as dwelling in the heart, writing His law there, as in Jeremiah 31:33; Ezekiel 11:19; 18:31; 36:26; but, none the less, that blessed brightness is destined yet to break out, as it did in the transfiguration of Christ, and as it will, in Him and in us, when we meet 'in the air' (1 Thess. 4:17).

One of the most important lessons of the passage is that it is none less than Almighty God Himself in His fullest integrity who institutes these perfect judgments. We may not wisely praise Him for them while we are in mortal bodies, susceptible as we are to carnal vindictiveness, but we shall one day, when we see how perfect His judgments are. 'Oh the depth of the riches and wisdom and knowledge of God! How unsearchable are his judgments and how inscrutable his ways!' (Rom. 11:33) Yes, but the transparency of the glass seems to suggest that one day they will be perfectly clear to us, too!

CHAPTER SIXTEEN

The Seven Bowls of Wrath
16:1-21

¹Then I heard a loud voice from the temple telling the seven angels, 'Go and pour out on the earth the seven bowls of the wrath of God.' Remember the plagues of Egypt!

²So the first angel went and poured his bowl on the earth, whence arose the second beast, representing false religion and philosophy (see Rev. 13:11); but look further back to 8:7, where the judgment of the trumpet which warned touched only a third of the earth: here there is no mention of a 'third'; *and foul and evil sores came upon the men who bore the mark of the beast and worshipped its image.* It may instantly occur to us, in view of the holiness and perfection of the judgments of the wrath of God, that the very introduction of what is foul bespeaks the inherent filth of the creatures visited. There could be nothing in the pure judgments of God to produce foul effects. These could only be the product of their own evil hearts brought out by the true judgments of God, just as medicine may produce suppuration. In a sense, the leprosy which broke out upon the forehead of irreverent Uzziah (2 Chron. 26:19)—and, indeed, on Miriam (Num. 12:10)—was not only judgment for sin, but evidence of sin already there. In that sense, sin is its own judgment. God simply commands it to expose itself and be banished to its own place.

³The second angel poured his bowl into the sea, whence arose the first beast representing wordly government (13:1), *and it became like the blood of a dead man, and every living thing died that was in the sea.* Compare with 8:8.

⁴The third angel poured his bowl into the rivers and the fountains of water, and they became blood. Cf 8:10, 11. *⁵And I heard the angel of water say, 'Just art thou in these thy judgments, thou who art and wast, O Holy One. ⁶For men have shed the blood of saints and prophets, and thou hast given them blood to drink. It is their due!' ⁷And I heard the altar cry, cf* 6:9–11 *'Yea, Lord God the Almighty, true and just are they judgments!'*

Note the finality of these judgments compared with those in chapter 8, where a third only is hurt. Hence the cry in verses 5–7 not only attributes the judgments to God (see Rom. 12:19), but regards them as just, due and final, in the sense that those judged have had their last chance. Doubtless the care with which the altar cry is made is intended to vindicate the awful inevitability of judgment when the last appeal has been made to men without response.

⁸The fourth angel poured his bowl on the sun, and it was allowed to scorch men with fire; ⁹men were scorched by the fierce heat, and they cursed the name of God who had power (authority) *over these plagues, and they did not repent and give him glory. Cf* the partial judgment in 8:12.

It may be remarked that the counterpart of these plagues is to be found in, *eg* Deuteronomy 28:22. But those were clearly disciplinary judgments upon God's own people, whereas these are 'terminal' judgments meted out upon those 'who bore the mark of the beast and worshipped its image.' (v.2) It may also be remarked that these terminal judgments are related to the preceding warning (trumpet) judgments (chapter 8), as the last plague upon Egypt (the death of the first-born along with the destruction of Pharaoh and his host in the Red Sea) was related to the earlier warning plagues. Other examples of warning judgments leading to final judgments in the Old Testament are found in the 'woes' in the prophetic books, *eg* Isaiah chapters 12–23; Jeremiah chapters 46—51; Ezekiel chapters 27–33, 38, 39; Amos chapters 1.2.1–3; Obadiah.

¹⁰The fifth angel poured his bowl on the throne of the beast, and its kingdom was in darkness; men gnawed their tongues in anguish ¹¹and cursed the God of heaven for their pains and sores, and did not repent of their deeds. The beast is

obviously the first beast of 13:1, representing evil government, the second beast (13:11), representing false religion
and philosophy, is later called the 'false prophet' (16:13;
19:20; 20:10). This bowl represents the final overthrow of
monstrous regimes in which man, from ancient Pharaoh to
Hitler, Stalin and Mao Tse Tung, has exalted himself over
his fellows (even aspiring to God's throne!), and has been
cast down; see Isaiah chapter 14 and Ezekiel chapter 28.
Men who have put their trust in these horrid emperors have
gone down into ungodly ruin.

[12]*The sixth angel poured his bowl on the great river
Euphrates, and its water was dried up, to prepare the way for
kings from the east.* [13]*And I saw, issuing from the mouth of
the dragon and from the mouth of the beast and from the
mouth of the false prophet, three foul spirits like frogs;* [14]*for
they are demonic spirits, performing signs, who go abroad to
the kings of the whole world, to assemble them for battle on
the great day of God the Almighty.* This sequence of bowls,
like the sequence of warning trumpets, has extended from
those wearing the mark of the beast relative to the earth,
sea, rivers, sun, and throne of the beast (a chief seat of evil
government) to the demonic spirits controlling such
persons, see *eg* Daniel 10:13, 20; Ephesians 6:12.

But what of the judgment on these demons? Have successive waves of these evil creatures been chained in darkness
(2 Pet. 2:4; Jude 6) since the particular emperor and empire
they sponsored finally fell? We do not know; but the judgments on these realms are here represented in terms of
Media and Persia taking over the huge but crumbling might
of Babylon (Euphrates), since Babylon is the representative biblical name for all evil rule from Genesis 11:9 to the
last ungodly government; see 17:5; 18:2, 10, 21. And
although all these judgments are set out in sequence, it is
suggested by the interpretation that they are taking place
throughout the gospel ages. Yet there is a climax, as is clear
from the reference to Armageddon in verse 16. See
Zechariah 12:11; Daniel 11:45; Ezekiel 39:11–20.

[15]*('Lo, I am coming like a thief!* See Matthew 24:43; 1
Thessalonians 5:2, 4; 2 Peter 3:10; Revelation 3:3. *Blessed is
he who is awake, keeping his garments that he may not go*

naked and be seen exposed!') Our Lord's coming is described as a 'thief in the night' in reference to His people's watchfulness and to those who keep awake (Matt. 25:1–13), and who keep their garments that is, those who maintain their supernatural covering of justification and sanctification because they are dressed in the robes of Christ's righteousness (Isa. 61:10; 2 Cor. 5:21b). 1 John 2:28 expresses this: 'And now, little children, abide in him, so that when he appears we may have confidence and not shrink back from him in shame at his coming.' This refers to any measure of self-trust which exposes our nakedness in the sight of God (see Rev. 3:18), however we or others mistakenly think we may cover ourselves with our own self-righteousness.

[16]*And they assembled them at the place which is called in Hebrew Armageddon* It is sufficient to say of Armageddon that it represents the Almighty's final clash with evil government; see Ezekiel chapters 38.39.

[17]*The seventh angel poured his bowl into the air, and a great voice came out of the temple, from the throne, saying, 'It is done!'* [18]*And there were flashes of lightning, loud noises, peals of thunder, and a great earthquake such as had never been since men were on the earth, so great was that earthquake.* [19]*The great city was split into three parts, and the cities of the nations fell, and God remembered great Babylon,* which means the spirit and evil principle of Babylon, in both human and demonic forms, *to make her drain the cup of the fury of his wrath.* [20]*And every island fled away, and no mountains were to be found;* see Zechariah 14:4, 10, which may mean that there is no escape or shelter for the denizens of these evil cities; [21]*and great hailstones, heavy as a hundredweight, dropped on men from heaven* (Josh. 10:11), *till men cursed God for the plague of the hail, so fearful was that plague.* We may compare this tremendous passage with similar climactic passages in the various sections of the book; *eg* 6:12–17; 11:19; 14:17–20; 19:11–21.

CHAPTER SEVENTEEN

The Harlot, Babylon
17:1–18

This is the penultimate section, chapters 17—19, in which the judgment of Babylon is fully and finally revealed. Chapter 17 tells the history of the spirit of Babylon (which goes back to Babel in Genesis ch. 11), chapter 18 her final downfall; and chapter 19, after the final banishment of the beast and false prophet, the heavenly rejoicing at Babylon's destruction.

A suitable superscription for this section would be from 1 John 2:17: 'And the world passes away, and the lust of it.' The final, terminal, 'last chance' judgments throughout the gospel ages having been unfolded generally in chapters 15 and 16, almost a whole section is now devoted to the overflow of the spirit of Babylon, beginning in chapter 17 with an analysis of the nature of that spirit.

The symbol of the worldly spirit is the scarlet woman, seated upon the scarlet beast symbolising the spirit of persecution. She is also seated on many waters (nations) which she influences (vv.1, 2), as a spirit of false allurement, seduction and enticement, which, as the spirit of city life, especially the great metropolises, beguiles and fascinates men. Such cities, and the spirit prevailing in them, have destroyed more human souls than tongue can tell. And it is appropriate, therefore, that one of the seven angels who bore the seven bowls of God's final wrath should be John's guide in a conducted review of that spirit's history. The opposite of this spirit is the Spirit of Wisdom in Proverbs chapter 8, and that of Israel as the wife of Jehovah, and the Church as the Bride of Christ.

¹Then one of the seven angels who had the seven bowls came and said to me, 'Come, I will show you the judgment of the great harlot who is seated upon many waters,' See verse 15: these waters represent nations refusing the headship of God—civilised man apart from God (see Gen. 4; Rom. 1:18–32): they are world powers symbolised by harlots, *eg* Tyre (Is. 23:16f); Nineveh (Nah. 3:4), whose influence we see, temporarily, even in the people of God when they are unfaithful to Him (Is. 1:21; Jer. 2:20; 3:1, 9; Ezek. 16:15, 32; Hos. 2:5). Note that a harlot is a whore, which is worse than an adulteress!

²'with whom the kings of the earth have committed fornication, and with the wine of whose fornication the dwellers on earth have become drunk.' By characterising the spirit of seduction as a woman, we see that behind and beyond great kings and emperors, there is a prevailing spirit which descends and settles upon great cities and entices men irresistibly, as wanton women do, mesmerising and spell-binding them; see Proverbs 2:12–19; 5:7. That spirit is well spoken of also as wine, for it is an intoxicating spirit which carries men away from their true selves until they live for what, ironically and perversely affords them decreasing satisfaction; and yet the craving increases, until the sheer, diabolical perversity of the evil spirit is exposed to all who have eyes to see.

³And he carried me away in the Spirit into a wilderness, here is heaven's estimate of the place where seduction dwells, and of the spirit which she thinks reigns there, *and I saw a woman, contra* 12:1, *sitting on a scarlet beast,* see the 'red' dragon, 12:3, 'red' sin, Isaiah 1:18, *which was full of blasphemous names, and it had seven heads and ten horns.* See on 12:3; these are powers accorded her by the dragon. The blasphemous names indicate that evil cannot but be preoccupied with names which inevitably remind it of its unwilling subservience to Almighty God. Its inferiority betrays itself in the bitterness of its blasphemies.

⁴The woman was arrayed in purple and scarlet, and bedecked with gold and jewels and pearls, this is the world of ungodly enchantment as blinded men see it, *holding in her hand a golden cup full of abominations and the impurities of her fornication;* the real nature of wickedness, albeit in a golden cup; *⁵and on her forehead was written a name of mystery: 'Babylon the great, mother of harlots and of earth's abominations.'* Note, she appears to be 'great' to eyes not opened to the true nature of the mystery, see 1 Samuel 16:7. Juvenal describes how the empress Messalina used to serve as a prostitute in a common brothel, and Seneca called Rome 'a filthy sewer'. Barclay comments, 'John's picture of Rome is not in the least exaggerated; it is actually restrained in comparison with some of the pictures which the Romans themselves drew of their civilisation.' (Quoted by Morris, p.207).

⁶And I saw the woman, drunk with the blood of the saints and the blood of the martyrs of Jesus. When I saw her, I marvelled greatly. There are two pictures here. The woman holds the golden cup full of abominations, being filled up, as the cup of God's wrath, to be poured out upon the wicked; see Isaiah 51:17, 22; Jeremiah 25:15, 17, 28; 51:7; Ezekiel 23:31–33; Revelation 14:10; 16:19; 18:6. But see the judgment also in terms of Isaiah 34:5–7: it is while the woman and her dupes have been filling up the cup of God's wrath that they have also been draining the cup of the martyrs' blood. How awful that the suffering and death of God's choicest servants is one 'item' only on the 'menu' of these abominable degenerates. This is how far human 'dogs' and 'swine' will go in trampling the holy things of God; see Matthew 7:6.

⁷But the angel said to me, 'Why marvel? Those who know the meaning of wickedness from the heavenly point of view, and its end, are not surprised at anything it can do, nor at its impressiveness. *I will tell you the mystery of the woman, and of the beast,* one mystery, *with seven heads and ten horns that carries her. ⁸The beast that you saw was, and is not, and is to ascend from the bottomless pit and go to perdition; and the dwellers on earth whose names have not been written in the book of life from the foundation of the world, will marvel to behold the beast, because it was and is not and is to come. ⁹This calls for a mind with wisdom: the seven heads are seven hills on which the woman is seated;* [10]*they are also seven kings, five of whom have fallen, one is, the other has not yet come, and when he comes he must remain only a little while.'*

Before we seek further elucidation of the mysteries of this passage, we must acknowledge the explanation given, weighing their disclosure, although they raise further questions. Contrast 'was and is not and is to come' with 'is and was and is to come' of 1:4, 8 (or 'was and is and is to come' of 4:8); the latter sustained and cumulative, the former fitful, bespeaking the restlessness of evil on the prowl to gain the greatest advantage possible in the disastrous situation it has created. The reference to the 'bottomless pit' (Greek, 'abyss') and 'perdition' ('destruction') should be compared with 20:3, 7, 10, 13–15: the 'pit' or 'abyss' is a temporary prison for evil spirits (*cf* 1 Pet. 3:19); whereas 'destruction' or 'the lake of fire' represents eternal destiny and desert.

Note that 'is not, and is to ascend' is less lurid than the version of the idea at 13:3, which has caused scholars to resort to the 'redivivus' myth of Nero (see notes on 13:3) as the original of the theme of resurgence of evil genius in other men in other days. The reason why dwellers on earth, whose names are not written in the book of life, marvel at the resurgence of the beast, is that they think that that spirit will go on for ever. Not so; the beast will go at last into perdition. This is a word of comfort to the Lord's own; evil in all its forms will have an end.

The wisdom which the mystery of the beast calls for does not see the revelation granted to John as dealing with individual historic personalities, but with types of men animated by particular evil spirits. The seven hills upon which Rome is built (some of these hills have been obliterated by the debris and rebuilding of centuries, *cf* the rising levels in Jerusalem), and on which the woman is seated, simply instance the current historic example at the time of writing.

The same interpretation goes for verse 10. The seven cited as emperors would be Augustus Caesar, Tiberius, Caligula, Claudius, Nero (Galba, Otho, Vitellius), Vespasian and Titus. But if, as Hendriksen suggests, we take them to be empires, they would be Old Babylonia, Assyria, Babylon,

Medo-Persia, Greece, Rome, and that which is to come—and for that, we could add any subsequent current, or coming empire!

[11]*'As for the beast that was and is not, it is an eighth but it belongs to the seven, and it goes to perdition.'* The eighth can only be the final antichrist himself, whose spirit is even now abroad, as John says, see 1 John 2:18; 4:3; 2 John 7.

[12]*And the ten horns that you saw are ten kings who have not yet received royal power, but they are to receive authority as kings for one hour, together with the beast.'* If the seven kings represent the *spirit* of the beast in empires, the ten kings may represent the *spirit* of the beast in emperors. The meaning of verse 12 will then be that the ten represent the short-lived reigns of men, who may be surprised at how quickly and easily they gain the ascendant, and may be equally surprised at how soon they are put down or fade away, not knowing that they are energised for their brief day of the beast, of whom they are successive 'incarnations'! See Luke 9:7–9; Malachi 4:5. Hendriksen says, 'All the mighty ones of this earth in every realm: art, education, commerce, industry, government, inasfar as they serve the central authority, are indicated. Self-aggrandisement *in opposition to Christ* is their goal. In order to reach this goal they are willing to give their power and authority to be beast.' (*More than Conquerors*, p.205).

[13]*'These are of one mind and give over their power and authority to the beast';* This is possible only because the beast, who is an evil spirit, inhabits these men, and, as in a diabolic religion, inspires them to surrender their powers to the spirit animating them, because they falsely think it is their own spirit. ('Then Satan entered into Judas Iscariot' [Lk. 22:3a], which can only mean that Judas betrayed Jesus and procured His death thinking that it was by his own act; but the deed being done, it appears that Satan allowed him to know by what power he had done it, whereupon Judas could not bear to continue in life, and went and hanged himself.)

[14]*'they will make war on the Lamb, and the Lamb will conquer, for he is Lord of lords and King of kings* (Deut. 10:17) *and those with him are called and chosen and faithful.'*

Note that the Lamb's own are 'with him'; for they are active, see 12:10, 11. Here is the implacable hostility of the nether spirit-world to Christ, characterised as the One who saves God's chosen and faithful from perdition by the shedding of precious blood. The victory proclaimed so serenely is categorical, there is no dubiety about it; for the Lamb is the Lion (5:5, 6), and the Lord of lords and King of kings: He is eternal deity, God (Heb. 1:8); whereas the other beings are His creatures. The struggle is unequal, and the ascendancy assured, even when as Man He assumed human vulnerability in order to save His own. They are His chosen ones, whom He inspires with the gift of His own faith, which He bestows on them (Eph. 2:8; Phil. 1:29a).

[15]*And he said to me, 'The waters that you saw* (17:1), *where the harlot is seated, are peoples and multitudes and nations and tongues.* [16]*And the ten horns that you saw, they and the beast will hate the harlot; they will make her desolate and naked, and devour her flesh and burn her up with fire,* [17]*for God has put it into their hearts to carry out his purpose by being of one mind and giving over their royal power to the beast, until the words of God shall be fulfilled.* [18]*And the woman that you saw is the great city which has dominion over the kings of the earth.'*

Note that the scarlet woman, representing worldly seduction and intoxication ('wine', v.2), is seated, on the one hand, on the waters of peoples, and, on the other, on the beast. She does not please the beast (to put it mildly) with her seducing performance, and we begin to see the final truth about those evil powers which seem so united against the Christ; amongst them there is ultimately no agreement—as with thieves! See historical examples of how this works on the human level: Judges 7:22; 1 Samuel 14:20; 2 Chronicles 20:23. See also Revelation 6:4, and Matthew 12:22–26. In the latter reference Jesus gives a hint of the essential and ultimate disunity and quarrelsomeness of all evil beings.

CHAPTER EIGHTEEN

The Fall of Babylon
18:1–24

We now come to the downfall of those imbued with the spirit of Babylon, whose history has been displayed in chapter 17. Chapter 18 has been characterised as a series of doom-songs, or poetic dirges, using the language of the Old Testament prophets.

¹*After this I saw another angel coming down from heaven having great authority; and the earth was made bright with his splendour.* cf Ezekiel 43:2. ²*And he called out with a mighty voice, 'Fallen, fallen is Babylon the great!* cf the fall of Tyre (Ezekiel chs.26–28); Babylon (Isaiah chs.13, 14, 21, Jeremiah chs. 50, 51); Ninevah (Nahum). *It has become a dwelling place* (a hold) *of demons, a haunt of every foul spirit, a haunt* (cage) *of every foul and hateful bird;* see Isaiah 13:1, 19–22; Jeremiah 50:39; 51:37; Zephaniah 2:14–15; ³*for all nations have drunk the wine of her impure passion* (14:8), *and the kings of the earth have committed fornication with her, and the merchants of the earth have grown rich with the wealth* (abundance) *of her wantonness.'* Notice the specific reason for her downfall: 'her impure passion.'

⁴*Then I heard another voice from heaven saying, 'Come out of her, my people, lest you take part in her sins, lest you share in her plagues;* note 'my people': cf Abram leaving Ur (Gen. 12:1); Lot leaving Sodom (Gen. 19:12); Israel departing from Korah and company (Num. 16:23, 24); Israel from Babylon (Is. 48:20; 52:11; Jer. 50:8; 51:6, 45; Zech. 2:6; see also 2 Cor. 6:14, 17; Eph. 5:11; 1 Tim. 5:22); these cannot be identified

123

with any of those kings, merchants or sea captains who stand back from Babylon in her destruction and lament her. There is no repentance there. *⁵for her sins are heaped high as heaven, and God has remembered her iniquities.'* See Galatians 6:7.

⁶'Render to her as she herself has rendered, and repay her double for her deeds; mix a double draught for her in the cup she mixed.' See Isaiah 40:2b. Morris says this is not revenge, but just requital; but he goes on to say that the simple "'eye for an eye and a tooth for a tooth', the lex talionis is not sufficient." Philip says, 'Mix her a drink of double strength!' But what does that mean? Jeremiah 16:18 implies double payment, although D. J. Wiseman says that then 'God is stigmatised as unreasonable and unjust.' However, see Exodus 22:4, 7; Isaiah 40:2, which seems to be saying something different from Jeremiah 50:15, 29. Can 'double' ever mean merely 'double back' in the sense of only full payment?

⁷'As she glorified herself and played the wanton, so give her a like measure of torment and mourning. Since in her heart she says, 'A queen I sit, I am no widow, mourning I shall never see,' see Isaiah 47:5–9, *⁸so shall her plagues come in a single day, pestilence and mourning and famine, and she shall be burned with fire; for mighty is the Lord God who judges her.'* See Isaiah 47:10, 11.

⁹And the kings of the earth, who committed fornication and were wanton with her, will weep and wail over her when they see the smoke of her burning (17:16); *¹⁰they will stand far off, in fear of her torment, and say, 'Alas! alas! thou great city, thou mighty city, Babylon! In one hour has thy judgment come.'*

¹¹And the merchants of the earth weep and mourn for her, since no one buys their cargo any more, Morris says, 'None is depicted as loving the city for herself, but only for what they could get out of her.' (p.218). *¹²cargo of gold, silver, jewels and pearls, fine linen, purple, silk and scarlet* (to Rome from China), *all kinds of scented wood,* 'citron wood', says Shewell-Cooper, *all articles of ivory, all articles of costly wood, bronze, iron and marble, ¹³cinnamon, spice, incense, myrrh, frankinscence, wine, oil, fine flour and wheat* (Egypt), cattle and sheep, horses and chariots, and slaves, that is human souls. 'They exchanged the persons of men and vessels of bronze for your merchandise.' (Ezek. 27:13).

[14]*'The fruit for which thy soul longed* (lusted) *has gone from thee, and all thy dainties,* oily, fatty things, *and thy splendour,* the Talmud says Rome had nine tenths of the world's wealth, *are lost to thee, never to be found again!'*

[15]*The merchants of these wares, who gained wealth from her, will stand far off, in fear of her torment, weeping and mourning aloud,* [16]*'Alas, alas, for the great city that was clothed in fine linen, in purple and scarlet, bedecked with gold, with jewels, and with pearls!* [17]*In one hour,* sudden, summary judgment! *all this wealth has been laid waste.' And all shipmasters and seafaring men, sailors and all whose trade is on the sea, stood afar off* [18]*and cried out as they saw the smoke of her burning, 'What city was like the great city?'* See Ezekiel 27:32. [19]*And they threw dust on their heads, as they wept and mourned, crying out, 'Alas, alas, for the great city where all who had ships at sea grew rich by her wealth! In one hour she has been laid waste.'*

[20]*'Rejoice over her, O heaven, O saints and apostles and prophets, for God has given judgment for you against her!'* See a different attitude here to Babylon's destruction from that of those above, the lamenting kings and merchants and sea-captains.

[21]*Then a mighty angel took up a stone like a great millstone and threw it into the sea,* see Jeremiah 51:63, 64, *saying, 'So shall Babylon the great city be thrown down with violence, and shall be found no more;* [22]*and the sound of harpers and minstrels, of flute players and trumpeters, shall be heard in thee no more;* see Exekiel 26:13; *and a craftsman of any craft shall be found in thee no more; and the sound of the millstone* preparing food, *shall be heard in thee no more;* [23]*and the light of a lamp shall shine in thee no more; and the voice of the bridegroom and bride shall be heard in thee no more;* see Jeremiah 7:34; *for thy merchants were the great men of the earth, and all nations were deceived by thy sorcery.'* See Nahum 3:4. We may say that here is described the final end of all that world of so-called culture and civilisation which started, alas, with the developments and advances in

civilised living of the wicked line of the Cainites (Gen. 4). For all its arts and crafts, the first examples of polygamy and murder took place there.

[24]*'And in her was found the blood of prophets and of saints, and of all who have been slain on earth.'* See Matthew 23:25–36. It is hard for worldlings to believe ill of this glorious worldly world of great cities with their splendour and wealth; but look what is in them! It is surely good and right for us to know and contemplate, without gloating and vindictiveness, that the sufferings of those who have endured for Christ's sake will be amply repaid to their tormentors, since 'Vengeance is mine, saith the Lord, I will repay' (Rom. 12:19).

CHAPTER NINETEEN

The Destruction of the Harlot and the Marriage Supper of the Lamb

19:1–21

Following the destruction of the worldly anti-Christian spirit of Babylon, the great multitude shout their praise with a threefold 'Hallelujah' in an almost unbelievably thunderous 'Niagara' of sound.

¹*After this I heard what seemed to be the mighty voice of a great multitude in heaven, crying, Hallelujah!* Praise the Lord! *Salvation and glory and power belong to our God,* ²*for his judgments are true and just* (15:3; 16:5); *he has judged the great harlot who corrupted the earth with her fornication* (Genesis chs. 4, 11), *and he has avenged on her the blood of his servants.'* (Rev. 6:10) ³*Once more they cried, 'Hallelujah! The smoke from her goes up,* that is, as an incense to the nostrils of the Almighty, bearing to Him the pure savour of the justice of the divine moral law, *for ever and ever.'*

T. F. Torrance says, 'The world likes a complacent, reasonable religion, and so it is always ready to revere some pale Galilean image of Jesus, some meagre anaemic Messiah, and to give Him a moderate rational homage.... The truth is that we have often committed adultery with alien ideologies, confounded the Gospel with the religions of nature, and imbibed the wine of pagan doctrines and false principles and deceitful practices. We have sought to bend the will of God to serve the ends of man, to alter the Gospel and shape the Church to conform to the fashions of the times. We have yielded to pride and to the lust for power. We have been intimidated by the might of the beast through society or the crowd or the state and betrayed again and again the cause of our Saviour.' (*The Apocalypse Today*, p.155) But not so any longer! Nor is the rejoicing negative, upon the destruction of Babylon, but positive upon the prospect of the Marriage Supper of the Lamb.

⁴*And the twenty-four elders and the four living creatures fell down and worshipped God who is seated on the throne, saying, 'Amen, Hallelujah!'* See Psalm 106:48. ⁵*And from the throne came a voice crying, 'Praise our God, all of you his servants, you who fear him, small and great.'*

⁶*Then I heard what seemed to be the voice of a great multitude, like the sound of many waters and like the sound of mighty thunder-peals, crying, 'Hallelujah! For the Lord our God the Almighty reigns.* Note that the former praise (vv.1–3) was for divine justice (15:3; 16:5; 19:1–3): now it is for Lordship. ⁷*Let us rejoice and exult and give him the glory* (Mark 2:19), *for the marriage of the Lamb has come, and his Bride has made herself ready';* see Ezekiel 16:8; Matthew 22:2; 25:1.

⁸*'It was granted her to be clothed with fine linen, bright and pure'—for the fine linen is the righteous deeds of the saints.* See Matthew 13:43; Ephesians 5:25–27; 2 Corinthians 11:2. Morris says, 'This is usually understood in the sense 'the righteous deeds of the saints' (RSV). But the word *dikaioma* never seems elsewhere to have the meaning 'righteous deeds'. It always denotes 'ordinance', or something of the kind. 'Sentence of justification' would be much more in accordance with New Testament usage…. This clothing is given to the saints. It is not provided by them. The white robes of the multitude in 7:9, 14 were not provided by any righteous acts on the part of the wearers, but were the result of washing in 'the blood of the Lamb'. So is it here.' (Morris, p.227) Charles says, 'The term *judgments (dikaiōmata)* is often understood in the sense 'righteous acts' (*eg* RV). But there is reason for holding that the term has to do with legal acts and we should understand it here of the 'judicial sentences of God in relation to the nations either in the way of mercy or condemnation.' (Quoted by Morris, p.190).

Morris' first quotation is hardly right: *dikaiōma* is certainly a righteous deed in Romans 5:18 (see Soutar's lexicon), albeit a deed of Christ. Also, see NEB Revelation 15:4: 'For thy just dealings stand revealed.' As to Charles' quotation, his is a strange way to read the plural *dikaiomata* and apply it to the nations!

The present writer believes this to be a crux for interpretation: to begin with, 'his Bride has made herself ready' is clear, definite and active, and the absolute 'givenness' of salvation is guarded by the words that follow at verse 9. How else are we to read the plural *dikaiōmata* than as deeds? And what of the doctrine of reward for works, so fully documented in the New Testament? See 1 Corinthians 3:10–15; 2 Corinthians 5:10; Revelation 22:11, 12; also the deeds of faith in James 2:18–26. Certainly Hendriksen is clear that 'the fine linen symbolises her righteous acts; hence her sanctified character, 7:13.' Of course, her righteousness is given. 'Her deeds have been washed by the blood of Christ.' *(More than Conquerors,* p.216) But they are wrought by her, none the less.

Evangelical scholars, so careful to attribute our whole salvation to Christ alone, seem unwilling to admit and concede the reality of the deeds of faith, for which the gift is given. Surely James 2:14–26 is the healthy corrective, as also, chapter 19:7 of the Westminster Confession of Faith, which deals fully with the many gracious uses of the Law for Christians during the gospel dispensation.

Further inquiry into the usage of the word *dikaiōma* yields interesting information. While it is generally agreed that the word normally means, a decree, law, sentence, or ordinance, Bagster's Greek lexicon gives as a first meaning, 'a rightful act', 'act of justice, equity', before the meaning, 'sentence'. See also the Septuagint (LXX) Greek for Genesis 26:5, 'kept my commandments', and for Exodus 15:26, 'keep his statutes'. Also, of the ten occurrences of the word in the New Testament, five, apart from our present text, speak of 'righteousness', or 'ordinances' as performed by men (Luke 1:6; Rom. 2:26: 8:4; Heb. 9:1, 10); two by Christ (Rom. 5:16, 18); two by God (Rom. 1:32; Rev. 15:4). Strong's Greek dictionary cites *dikaiōma* as 'an equitable deed'.

Concerning Romans 5:18, in a footnote John Murray says, 'Lightfoot adduces Revelation 15:4; 19:8 as examples of *dikaiōma* in the sense of 'righteous deed'. It is pointless for Godet to argue, in favour of the meaning, 'sentence of justification', that 'in Paul's terminology it is God and not Jesus who is *the justifier*.' 'The righteous act' of Christ does not refer to the sentence which, as Godet rightly observes, is the act of God as distinguished from Christ, but to the righteousness of Christ's obedience and is parallel to *hupakoè* (obedience) in verse 19.' Evidently supporting this view of *dikaiōma* as an act, Murray says, 'On the meaning of *dikaiōma* cf the fine treatment by G. Schrenk in *Theologisches Worterbuch zum Neuen Testament, ad loc.*' (*The New London Commentary on the New Testament*, p.200)

Perhaps we ought to let Hendriksen conclude the matter: 'This feast is the climax of that entire process by means of which the Bridegroom, Christ, comes to His bride, the church. It is the goal and purpose of that ever-increasing intimacy, union, fellowship, and communion between the Redeemer and the redeemed.' (*More than Conquerors*, p.216)

⁹*And the angel said to me, 'Write this: Blessed are those who are invited* (called) *to the marriage supper of the Lamb.' And he said to me, 'These are true words of God.'* The emphasis is upon the word 'blessed'. All that is said is true, being words of God; but, particularly, that those called to the Supper are to be blessed. John is so overawed by the prospect, impressively stated by the angel, that he feels like bowing down and worshipping the heavenly being.

¹⁰*Then I fell down at his feet to worship him, but he said to me, 'You must not do that!* There is, of course prostration before angels in the Old Testament (Num. 22:31; 1 Chron. 21:16), but surely in homage, not in worship. Some were tempted to worship angels at Colosse (Col. 2:18), which may have had something to do with the beginnings of the Gnostic heresy. *I am a fellow servant with you*, see Hebrews 1:13, 14; 1 Corinthians 6:3, *and your brethren who hold the testimony of Jesus. Worship God.'* (Matt. 4:10) Note how theocentric (God-centred) this is: not, 'Worship Jesus,' although Jesus is God (Heb 1:8) and no one honours the Father like the Son. Jesus Himself calls His Father 'God' (Matt. 27:46), and His Spirit teaches the apostle Paul to call the Father 'the God of our Lord Jesus Christ'; see also Ephesians 1:3, 17; Romans

15:6; 2 Corinthians 1:3; 11:31; Colossians 1:3; 1 Peter 1:3. Note also that the order of the Persons of the Trinity is jealously guarded by Scripture, and we ought to observe that order with great care. Not only so, but in handing down holy things from God to men, the order of those involved in handing them down is also important; *eg* in Revelation 1:1–3, trace the order from the Father to John; or, in the case of the giving of the Law, the Law was handed down from God, through angels, to Moses, and thence to Israel; see Galatians 3:19; Deuteronomy 33:2 (Greek, not Hebrew); Psalm 68:17; Acts 7:38, 53; Hebrews 2:2; see also Paul's testimony to the holy tradition given to him (1 Cor. 15:3; 2 Tim. 3:14–17). The angel's point seems to be that we are to trace back everything purporting to come from God through every intermediary to the Son, and thence to the Father (1 Cor. 15:28).

For the testimony of Jesus is the spirit of prophecy. The connecting 'for' introduces the reason why John must not worship angels. They are witnesses in a category akin to that of men (the prophets) which is a category radically different from Jesus' own witness to His Father. The 'testimony of Jesus' (see 1:2, 9; 6:9; 12:17; 20:4), is first the testimony He bore by His incarnation and work to the Father's will and purpose: it is then the testimony of men and angels to the witness of Christ to His Father; and it is thus the 'spirit of prophecy'.

[11]*Then I saw heaven opened* (4:1), *and behold, a white horse!* (6:2) *He who sat upon it is called Faithful and True* (1:5; 3:7, 14), *and in righteousness he judges and makes war.* This is undoubtedly Christ. [12]*His eyes are like a flame of fire*, see also Daniel 7:9; 10:6; Revelation 1:14; 2:18, *and on his head are many diadems; He is King* of kings; *and he has a name inscribed which no one knows but himself.* But John proceeds to tell us that the name is The Word of God. What does it mean? That Christ, the equal Son of God, alone knows the Father (Matt. 11:27) and can fully and worthily communicate God's Word; for the Word of God in its fulness can be nothing less than God incarnate communicating the divine Word, personally. The challenge of the angel therefore seems to be, that alleged communications from God are

to be authenticated *eg* by tracing them back to the Godhead by following His lines of communication (see John 8:12–59); or that they are substantiated by the coming to pass of their predictive prophecies (*eg* Deut. 18:15–22, 2 Chron. 18:16, 33, 34) and are therefore seen to be from God. The unknown element in the name undoubtedly belongs to the impenetrable mystery of the blessed Trinity; see John 1:1, 18; Romans 8:27; 1 Corinthians 2:10b, 11, 16.

[13]*He is clad in a robe dipped in blood*, this is not the blood of the cross, but that of His enemies: for the fierceness of the wrath of God, see, *eg* Isaiah 63:1–6; Jeremiah 25:15, 16, 27–29; Revelation 14:20; *and the name by which he is called is The Word of God.* [14]*And the armies of heaven*, angelic armies, *arrayed in fine linen, white and pure*, holy angels, *followed him on white horses.*

[15]*From his mouth issues a sharp sword with which to smite the nations*, for 'sword' see Genesis 3:24; Exodus 17:13; Joshua 5:13; Isaiah 34:5–7; Jeremiah 25:16, 27, 29; Matthew 10:34; Revelation 1:16; 2:12, 16; 6:4, 8; 19:21; *and he will rule* (shepherd) *them with a rod of iron* (2:27; 12:5); *he will tread the wine press* (Is. 63:3; Rev. 14:19–20), *of the fury of the wrath of God the Almighty.* See Isaiah 13:13; Jeremiah 50:13, 15; Revelation 16:19; also Isaiah 34:2; 51:17–23; Jeremiah 30:23, 24; Micah 5:15; Nahum 1:1–3; Romans 1:18. [16]*On his robe and on his thigh he has a name inscribed, King of kings and Lord of lords.* *cf* 17;14: Charles says the name is revealed under His streaming garment.

Now follows the overthrow of the beast and the false prophet. [17]*Then I saw an angel standing in the sun, and with a loud voice he called to all the birds that fly in mid-heaven* (8;13; 14:6), *'Come, gather for the great supper of God*, contrast the supper of the Lamb, verse 9, [18]*to eat the flesh of kings, the flesh of captains, the flesh of mighty men, the flesh of horses and their riders, and the flesh of all men, both free and slave, both small and great.'* Note, that vast distinctions on earth have no significance in moral and spiritual terms. Morris remarks that the 'overthrow of evil' is now seen to be 'total', but he is excluding the devil himself, for he is not dealt with finally until chapter 20.

This passage is taken from the sequence in Ezekiel,

chapters 38 and 39, which deal prophetically with the final battle of Armageddon against Gog and Magog; see especially 39:4, 17–20. Note, that the implication of many divine judgments is that one evil swallows another (*cf* Babylonia consuming Assyria; Persia, Babylonia; Greece, Persia; Syria and Egypt, Greece; and Rome, all others) until all evil is consigned, first to the abyss, God's temporary prison, then the abyss with its prisoners is cast into the lake of fire, God's final and eternal 'incinerator' of evil; see Chapter 20.

[19]*And I saw the beast* (2 Thess. 2:7, 9–12) *and the kings of the earth with their armies gathered to make war against him who sits upon the horse and against his army.* This is the battle of Armageddon; see 2 Thessalonians 2:8 and Revelation 20:7–10, where the battle is described in relation to Satan. This final battle is also dealt with, in different aspects, towards the end of the preceding sections, 6:12–17; 11:15–19; 14:14–20; 16:17–21. Here it is described in terms of the final overthrow of the beast.

[20]*And the beast* (13:1; 16:13; 17:3, 7) *was captured and with it the false prophet* (13:11; 16:13; 20:10) *who in its presence had worked the signs by which he deceived those who had received the mark of the beast and those who worshipped its image.* Note the false prophet's treachery to his devotees! *These two were thrown alive*, they have the same unending torment as those they deceived, see 14:9–11, *into the lake of fire that burns* with brimstone. See 20:10, 15; Daniel 12:2; Matthew 3:12; 18:8; 25:46; John 5:29; Acts 24:15. [21]*And the rest were slain by the sword of him who sits upon the horse, the sword that issues from his mouth*; that is to say, it is the sword of the Word of God (*cf* v.13); *and all the birds were gorged with their flesh.*

Note that, to the end, evil swallows evil (see 2 Chronicles 20:23) until all is cast into God's final and eternal repository for it; and this is done primarily that heaven may be perfectly pure and holy.

CHAPTER TWENTY

The Last Judgment
20:1–15

We now come to the final section of the book, in which the ultimate battle between good and evil is rehearsed for the last time in terms of Satan's destruction, the beast and the false prophets already having been dealt with. After this, the main subject to the end is the bliss and glory of the saints with God in Christ.

Those who question Hendriksen's interpretation of the Revelation, as a recurring rehearsal of the long age between the first and second comings of our Lord, may find the following comparisons of chapters 11, and 12—14 with chapter 20, helpful.

Rev. 12:5–12:
Following Christ's victory, Satan is hurled down.

Rev. 11:2–6. 14ff
A long period of powerful witness by the church.

Rev. 11:7; 13:7:
A brief period of persecution.

Rev. 11:17–18; 14:14ff:
The Second Coming.

Rev. 20:1–3:
Satan is bound and his power curbed while the church conquers by evangelising.

Rev. 20:2–3:
The same.

Rev.20:7–8:
The same.

Rev. 20:11ff:
The same.

The present writer owning his arrival at a view of the last things which does justice to the sequence of events predicted in Romans 11, would like to say that he has come to it after fifty years of earnest search for the truth, twenty-five years accepting the pre-millennial viewpoint that Christ returns before the millennium; then twenty-five years accepting the a-millennial viewpoint which purposes to deny any millennium but actually sees it as the time between Christ's two comings. It has seemed natural therefore to proceed to a position, which sees the coming of Christ towards the end of the age, following the conversions of natural Jewry and the consequent Gentile upsurge of faith as predicted in Romans 11:12, 15. This view however does not exclude the final apostasy as predicted in Ezekiel chs. 38, 39; Matthew 24 and Revelation 20:7–10.

Note here should be taken of a recent post-millennial interpretation of Revelation chapter 20 in a book by J. Marcellus Kik, *An Eschatology of Victory* (The Presbyterian and Reformed Publishing Co., 1974). Discussing the undoubted crux of chapter 20, 'the first resurrection' (v.5), he rejects the view that the 'souls' (v.4) are the disembodied spirits of departed saints. That state of disembodiment, he says, is 'not a resurrection'. The word 'souls', he avers, as so often, refers to the mortal lives of the saints on earth, and the first resurrection is undoubtedly the quickening of their souls in regeneration. Kik cites Colossians 2:12–13; Ephesians 2:1, 5, 6; 1 John 3:14 (he could have cited other references) for this quickening. But it has to be pointed out that in the significant passage in 1 Peter 3:18 the same word for 'quickening' is used of the translation of our Lord's spirit, after His mortal death. There is therefore a strong precedent for its use in this way in Revelation 20:4.

The question also arises: How many categories are enumerated in Revelation 20:4? Is it necessary to assume that those seated on thrones to whom judgment was committed—the souls of those beheaded for their testimony and those who had not worshipped the beast—all belong to one narrow and exclusive category, namely, disembodied martyrs? There seems no reason why the 'first resurrection' should not cover the regeneration of the saints as saved souls, and also the departed spirits of the saints with Christ, which are two successive conditions of the same category of persons. Thus the two resurrections are (1) the regeneration of souls (Eph. 2:1, 5; Col. 2:12, 13; 1 John 3:14), and (2) the resurrection of the bodies of both the wicked and the righteous (John 5:24–29) at Christ's coming.

¹Then I saw an angel coming down from heaven, holding in his hand the key of the bottomless pit, Greek, 'abyss', *and a great chain.* (2 Pet. 2:4; Jude 6) *²And he seized the dragon,* note the ease with which the devil is captured when his time has come, *that ancient serpent, who is the Devil and Satan* (12:9), *and bound him* (Matt. 12:29; Rev. 12:11; Matt. 4: 1–11; Lk. 10:17–18; Col. 2:15; Heb. 2:14) *for a thousand years, ³and threw him into the pit, and shut it and sealed it over him, that he should deceive the nations no more, till the thousand years were ended. After that he must be loosed for a little while.*

The thousand years (Latin, 'millennium') is the subject of endless discussion. According to the interpretation generally followed in this study there is no difficulty: the thousand years stand for the time between the two comings of Christ, described in the Revelation variously as 'forty-two months' (Rev. 11:2; 13:5), 'one thousand two hundred and sixty days' (Rev. 11:3; 12:6), 'a time, and times, and half a time' (Rev. 12:14), 'a thousand years' (Rev. 20:2–7).

We can understand the objection to this clear and simple view, since the word 'millennium' has been associated with a time of bliss, but there is no essential connection between the word and an ideal state. True, Satan is bound and cannot deceive the nations during that time, and certainly converts are constantly being made from all nations; but the thousand years have been equated with a paradisal state because the binding of Satan has been associated (wrongly, we believe) with his final not his potential overthrow. For Christ's victory over all evil by death and resurrection is final, but latent to the extent that it operates only by the exercise of faith (Matt. 12:29; Acts 4:12; Eph. 2:8; 1 John 5:4). This is perhaps the least understood gospel truth of all. Men, even Christian men, expect Christ's victory to achieve immediate results—often other results than those Christ died to gain for us by faith as appropriated and employed in this dispensation. But the victory is to faith only, to which all believers are 'shut up' (Gal. 3:22–26; also Deut. 30:14 and Rom. 10:8).

It may be asked: But are not the nations deceived now? The answer must be: Not as they will be towards the end of this age (see v.7). Although Satan in his bound state becomes increasingly desperate (12:12), he does not have the power at present which he will have hereafter. One of the immediate effects of the resurgence of evil then will be to show to men the extent of Satan's influence upon the world, his release at that time revealing the full effects of his malevolent power, as these are not known in this age.

⁴*Then I saw thrones, and seated on them were those to whom judgment was committed.* Of thirty-one references to the throne of God in the book of the Revelation, more than half refer to the saints dwelling and reigning with Christ, *eg* 3:21; 8:3; 14:3; 22:3. The thrones here are undoubtedly those of the redeemed; see Daniel 7:9, 10; Matthew 19:28; 20:21; 1 Corinthians 6:2, 3; Hebrews 2:5–16; Revelation 3:21.

But where are these thrones? Hendriksen says upon the basis of thirty-one references in the Revelation that they are in heaven, but then Paul tells the Ephesians that saints still in the body are seated with Christ in the heavenly places (*cf* also Gal. 3:1). The question posed by a post-millennial interpretation is: Are saints sitting upon thrones, as those to whom judgment is committed, necessarily in heaven? True, Paul's references in 1 Corinthians 6:2–3 to the saints judging the world, and angels, are both in the future tense, but does he necessarily mean after death? Certainly, a thorough study needs to be made of the authority vouchsafed to the saints, now, by virtue of their being seated with Christ in His place of victory at the right hand of the Father. Without being dogmatic, since it is safer to be tentative on matters pertaining to this vexed but important chapter than to close the mind to possible truth, we suggest that it is possible to think concerning verse 4 (and also concerning the 'first resurrection' in verses 5, 6) of two states of the redeemed; in the body, and out of it. At least, this permits us meantime to have the best of two worlds of interpretation!

Also I saw the souls of those who had been beheaded for their testimony to Jesus and for the word of God, and who had not worshipped the beast or its image and had not received its mark on their foreheads or their hands. It is monstrous exegesis of some post-millennialists to seek to force this statement into the category of souls still in their bodies! Surely it does violence to common sense. Nor can we believe that by inexorable logic the whole of verse 4 has to be forced into one narrow and rigid category, so that martyred souls only are referred to. Surely the elemental and final nature of the chapter with regard to evil forbids narrow classification. There is certainly danger in segregating categories of saints, as interpreters have discovered who, pressing distinctions too far, regard 'overcomers' (see AV Rev. 2:7; 3:21; 12:11; 21:7) as select groups of saints (*cf* G. H. Lang in his commentary on Hebrews).

Charles implies that the words beyond the connecting 'ands' in verse 4 merely explain what precedes, namely, that they are all and only martyred saints; but Swete thinks they may possibly introduce another class. Morris thinks not; but Hendriksen is sure that they do, and we subscribe to this view. It seems incredible that those referred to here (with 'those who conquer' in 2:7, 11, 17, 26; 3:5, 12, 21; 12:11; 21:7) are martyred saints only. The very words, 'the rest of the dead', v.5, suggest two categories of men, the redeemed, and those not redeemed.

Note that the saints are not only reigning with Christ, but worshipping God, see 1:6; 4:10; 5:9–10; 7:15; 14:4; 19:4; 22:3. *They came to life, and reigned with Christ a thousand years.* Against the assertion of post-millennialists that this can refer only to the new birth (*eg* Eph. 2:1, 5; Col. 2:12–13; 1 John 3:14) and that the translation of disembodied souls to heaven is not a resurrection, we have already cited 1 Peter 3:18, which states that our Lord's spirit was quickened when it left His mortal body. Marcellus Kik tries hard to minimise the force of scriptural references to the soul as disembodied, but see the Shorter Catechism (37), 'The souls of believers are at their death made perfect in holiness, and do immediately pass into glory; and their bodies, being still united to Christ, do rest in their graves till the resurrection'.

⁵*The rest of the dead did not come to life until the thousand years were ended. This is the first resurrection.* ⁶*Blessed and holy is he who shares in the first resurrection! Over such the second death (cf* 20:14; 21:8) *has no power, but they shall be priests of God and of Christ, and they shall reign with him a thousand years.* When verses 5 and 6 are taken together and the facts marshalled, the case for 'the rest of the dead' belonging to the elemental category of the lost is overwhelming; see John 5:28, 29; 11:25, 26. The words 'blessed' and 'holy', the undoubted reference to 'the priesthood of all believers,' on the one hand (see 1:6; 4:10; 5:10; 7:15; 14:4), and the implications that all others are involved in the second death on the other, surely assign the two classes to elementally opposite categories. Whatever variations of interpretative detail may be favoured for verses 4–6, there can be no reasonable doubt that the two elemental categories of the saved and the lost are here set over against each other.

⁷*And when the thousand years are ended, Satan will be loosed from his prison* ⁸*and will come out to deceive the nations which are at the four corners of the earth, that is, Gog and Magog,* see Ezekiel chapters 38, 39, to gather them for battle; *cf* 16:12–16; *their number is like the sand of the sea.* ⁹*And they marched up over the broad earth and surrounded the camp of the saints and the beloved city; cf* 17:14; *but fire came down from heaven and consumed them,* This final attack of the earthly forces of evil under Satan, liberated for a season, is naturally the greatest, most widespread and concentrated attack upon the saints of all time; see Matthew chapter 24; Mark 13:20; 2 Thessalonians 2:3–10; Revelation 11:9, 10; 16:12–16; 19:19.

¹⁰*and the devil who had deceived them was thrown into the lake of fire and brimstone where the beast and the false prophet were, and they will be tormented day and night for ever and ever.* This is the 'endless end' of the arch-fiend himself; *cf* 14:9–11. What can such a consummation be but the cause of unparalleled rejoicing to all who have been belaboured by the onslaughts of his hideous power. Now our highest thought is concentrated on praise of the greatness of God, who endured the contradiction of His enemy, the enemy

of God and man, in order to produce such rich fruits of redemption even unto eternal glory.

[11]*Then I saw a great white throne and him who sat upon it; from his presence earth and sky fled away, and no place was found for them.* No need to ask who is seated upon the great white throne: it is the Almighty Himself: it is the throne of God and of the Lamb; see Daniel 7:9, 10; Matthew 25:31ff; Romans 14:10; 2 Corinthians 5:10. The preparation for the last judgment is expressed in cosmic terms; see 6:12–17; 11:19; 16:18; and 2 Peter 3:10–12; also Isaiah 13:10; 34:4; Ezekiel 32:7; Daniel 7; Joel 2:10, 11, 30, 31; 3:15; Amos 8:9; Zephaniah 1:15; Acts 2:20.

[12]*And I saw the dead, great and small,* distinctions which may refer to worldly standards, although the comparison may be between potentials for evil, *standing before the throne,* this is inevitably the decisive moment for every man, when the author of evil, with his multiple and manifold deceptions, has been banished, *and books were opened.* See Daniel 7:10b. These books undoubtedly contain the records of every single human life. *Also another book was opened, which is the book of life.* See 3:5; 13:8. *And the dead were judged by what was written in the books, by what they had done.* See Matthew 16:27; Acts 10:42; 17:31; Romans 2:16; 14:10; 2 Corinthians 5:10; 11:15; Ephesians 6:8; Revelation 22:11–12.

[13]*And the sea gave up the dead in it;* the reference to those buried at sea is thought to emphasise the fact that every body of man, wheresoever laid, will be accounted for; *Death and Hades gave up the dead in them;* it is suggested that 'Death' is the fact and power of death, whereas 'Hades' is the state of separation of body from soul, which, although it could not hold our Lord (see Acts 2:24–28), has, nevertheless, held all men hitherto in its separating grip, *cf* 6:9–11; *and all were judged by what they had done.*

[14]*Then death* (1 Cor. 15:26) *and Hades were thrown into the lake of fire.* See John 5:25–29. *This is the second death,* see 2:11; 20:6; 21:8, *the lake of fire;* [15]*and if any one's name was not found written in the book of life, he was thrown into the lake of fire.*

CHAPTER TWENTY ONE

The New Heaven
and the New Earth
21:1–27

In view of the post-millennial interpretation of chapter 20 by J. Marcellus Kik, discussed above, it is perhaps fair to say here that he places chapters 21 and 22:1–5 within the present millennial kingdom which Christ will hand over to His Father (1 Cor. 15:24–28). After this, he says, the 'consummate state', a purely spiritual condition not at all described in Scripture, will begin. 'Revelation is concerned almost entirely with the Messianic kingdom which begins in time and ends in time...Revelation is completely silent as to what type of environment will be the enjoyment of the 'spiritual body'....The eschatology of the Old Testament is chiefly concerned with the Messianic kingdom and its types speak of the Messianic kingdom. The predictive and didactic elements of New Testament prophecy deal with the Messianic kingdom. The consummate kingdom is not the great object either of Old Testament prophecy or New Testament prophecy.' (Kik, *An Eschatology of Victory,* pp.17, 256).

The answer of Hendriksen the a-millennialist, to the assertion that none of Revelation chapters 21 and 22:1–5 describes the heavenly state, but the heavenly experience of the church on earth during the millennial kingdom, is that this is too radical. 'Now, Revelation 21:1—22:5 pictures what? The ideal church as it now is? Or, the universe and the church of the future? As we see it, neither of these answers is complete. We have in this section a description of that which is *ideal*. Whatever is the result of God's redeeming grace—whether in the present or in the future—is included here. This redeeming grace and transforming power of God must not be reviewed as pertaining only to the future. No, right now, in this present era, it is already working in the hearts of God's children. Accordingly, what we find here in Revelation 21:1—22:5 is a description of *the redeemed universe of the future as foreshadowed by the redeemed church of the present.' (More than Conquerors, p.237)*

¹Then I saw a new heaven and a new earth (Is. 65:17; 66:22; Matt. 19:28a; Acts 3:21; Rom. 8:19–22; 2 Pet. 3:13); *for the first heaven and the first earth had passed away, and the sea was no more.* Most writers agree that the sea here represents restlessness (Job 1:7; 2:2; Is. 57:20; Rev. 13:1; 16:3), tempest, cruelty; and, some say, separation.

The picture of the renewed and regenerate heaven and earth, the new paradise of God (2:7), must surely be compared with the original garden of Eden in Genesis. The paradise which man lost by the sin of disobedience and rebellion against the lavish goodness of God is now restored to him through the second, or last Adam, Christ. In the new paradise, the lights created by God at the first are no longer required (21:23). There is no evil one, such as seduced Adam and Eve (Gen. 3:1–6). Man is no longer fleeing in shame to hide from God (Gen. 3:7–12): God will now dwell with him in the most exquisite, intimate, blissful communion.

²And I saw the holy city, new Jerusalem—there is need of a *new* Jerusalem! (11:8)—*coming down out of heaven from God* (21:10), This is a remarkable emphasis, since we normally think of eternal blessedness in terms of ascent. The whole idea of a new earth has scarcely gripped the mind and imagination of the Christian church. It needs to do so, to provide correspondence with our earthly state and substance to our notions of heaven. *prepared* (19:8) *as a bride adorned for her husband* (Is. 61:10–11); We should be glad that Scripture provides so many rich pictures of the church in relation to Christ as the New Jerusalem (Is. 26:1; Ps. 48), as the Bride (2 Cor. 11:2; Rev. 21:9) and as the body of Christ (1

Cor. 12:27; Eph. 1:23; 4:12; Col. 1:18).

Throughout Scripture the location of Jerusalem affords fascinating allusions. The Bride, too, is the New Testament counterpart of the picture of Israel as the wife of Jehovah, of which there is an equal wealth of allusion throughout Scripture. And the body of Christ has been given a wonderful intimacy and illumination by the apostle Paul's anology of the human body in, *eg* 1 Corinthians 12:12–26. All this gives point to the affinity between Christ and His church (*cf* also Eph. 5:21–33). This is what John now writes about.

³*and I heard a great voice from the throne saying,* note how impressively the great announcement is signalled, *'Behold, the dwelling of God is with men. He will dwell with them, and they shall be his people,* or peoples, *and God himself will be with them';* some manuscripts add, 'and be their God.' This divine intention runs throughout Scripture as a theme, and sums up the Almighty's purpose in creation and redemption. It was for this that the counsels of the holy Trinity took place before the world began (Eph. 1:3–10), that God the Father might provide a worthy Bride for His eternal Son. This could be worthily accomplished only by placing (adopting) these creaturely-derived sons and daughters within the risen life of His Son the only begotten, thus making them worthy of their exalted station. This was possible only through their redemption from sin by Christ's blood.

We need to note that God saved us in Christ not merely to make us clean and holy, but because He purposed to betroth us to His Son, which purpose nothing in heaven, earth, or hell can frustrate. He wants us, because He wants us—because He wants us! see Deuteronomy 7:6–9. Note the following list of references to the oft-repeated declaration that God wants to dwell with us, and be our God, and us to be His 'peculiar' people (1 Pet. 2:9): Genesis 17:7–8; Exodus 19:6; 20:2; Leviticus 11:45; 26:12, 45; Deuteronomy 5:2, 3, 6; 10:15; Isaiah 43:21; Jeremiah 24:7; 30:22; 31:33; Ezekiel 11:20; 37:27; Zechariah 13:9. The number of such references in the New Testament is too numerous to cite. Practically the whole New Testament bears witness to God's desire to have a people for His own, and it describes the means by which it is fulfilled, in and by Christ. These may be summed up in Hebrews 2:11–13; 11:16.

[4]*'he will wipe away every tear from their eyes, and death shall be no more* (1 Cor. 15:26; Rev. 20:14), *neither shall there be mourning nor crying nor pain any more, for the former things have passed away.' cf* 7:13–17. Note that the eternal state of redeemed men is expressed here in terms of our present human life, but it is quite without fruit of sin, pain and suffering (Is. 25:8; 35:10; 51:11). These were the 'former things' resulting from the curse (Gen. 3:14–19; 1 Tim. 2:13–15; 1 Cor. 15:54–57). They are now reversed.

[5]*And he who sat upon the throne,* (never described, see 4:2; 5:1, *said, 'Behold, I make all things new.'* See Isaiah 42:9; 43:19; 48:6; 2 Corinthians 5:17. *Also he said, 'Write this, for these words are trustworthy and true.'* (22:6) [6]*And he said to me, 'It is done!' cf* 16:17.

Note, verse 6 reads curiously after verse 5. Charles suggests that 5c ('Also he said 'Write this, for these words are trustworthy and true.') is an interpolation, but it is surely better, with the NEB, to regard it as a parenthesis, and place it within brackets. 6a then follows naturally the words, 'Behold, I make all things new,' and the whole statement reads thus, '"Behold, I make all things new"…And he said to me, "It is done!"'

'I am the Alpha and the Omega, the beginning and the end.' These words are the first and last letters of the Greek language (in which Revelation was originally written). See also 1:8; 17c; 22:13. The expression seems to suggest that God who from eternity to eternity possesses absolute integrity and is consistent in all His acts, has completed at the end of time that for which time was created, namely, the consummation of His purpose by redemption and regeneration and by the re-constitution of all things; see Matthew 19:28; Acts 3:21. All this in the interests of the salvation of His people, because He cares for them and desires them to be with Him in His kingdom, in order that they may enjoy as a reward for their faithfulness to their Lord and Saviour the reverse of the privations and sufferings they endured in their earthly pilgrimage.

'To the thirsty I will give water without price, freely, (Rom.

3:23, 24), *from the fountain of the water of life.'* See Isaiah 12:3; 55:1; Matthew 5:6; John 4:10, 14; 7:37, 38. This figure for salvation was naturally a favourite with those who dwelt in a land of heat and great drought; nothing could possibly be so refreshing to a dry and thirsty soul as living and life-giving water. But that blessed figure has to be integrated with another, which seems to turn the notion of salvation from a rescue from death in a desert to that of salvation as a victory in war!

⁷*He who conquers* (Rom. 8:37; 1 John 5:4–5; Rev. 2:7, 11, 17, 26; 3:5, 12, 21) *shall have this heritage, and I will be his God and he shall be my son,'* See 2 Samuel 7:14a. This is the victory, and the life (John 17:2, 3), which is in fact the closest relationship possible with God through His Son, Jesus Christ.

The complete, final and utter contrast to this, in the great divide (Luke 16:26), is now described. ⁸*But as for the cowardly* (2 Tim. 1:7), *the faithless* (Rom. 14:23) *the polluted* (Rev. 21:27), *as for murderers* (Exod. 20:13; 1 John 3:15), *fornicators* (Exod. 20:14), *sorcerers* (Deut. 18:9–14), *idolators* (Exod. 20:3–6), *and all liars* (Exod. 20:16; Rev. 22:15), *their lot shall be in the lake that burns with fire and brimstone, which is the second death,'* (Rev. 20:14).

⁹*Then came one of the seven angels who had the seven bowls full of the seven last plagues* (15:6; 17:1), *and spoke to me, saying, 'Come I will show you the Bride, the wife of the Lamb.'* This is the only place where the church is called the 'wife' of the Lamb, but it is the climax of that 'love affair' which is the greatest romance in the world, the love of God for His people, so beautifully envisaged in the Scriptures (Ps. 45; Matt. 25:1; John 3:29; 2 Cor. 11:2; Eph. 5:21–32).

¹⁰*And in the Spirit he carried me away to a great, high mountain, and showed me the holy city Jerusalem coming down out of heaven from God,* ¹¹*having the glory of God,* this is the fulfilment of the total outreach of the love of God, that His chosen ones should show forth His glory. It must never be forgotten that *glory* is the ultimate essence of the being and character of Almighty God; this is what we share with God as creatures through redemption and the new birth: *its radiance like a most rare jewel, like a jasper, clear as crystal.*

"There is a City Bright - closed are its gates to sin ...

The most rare jewel is clearly what we call the diamond, not a coloured stone; for deep in the facets of its light, like the sun, are hid all the colours of the spectrum, and yet it is perfectly transparent, with the white light, purity, and holiness of Christ. That which will shine in heaven's glory as the brightest jewel in Christ's crown will be His people, His new Jerusalem, His Bride, His Wife, His Body.

The city itself will gleam with the white light of crystal walls: [12]*It had a great, high wall,* 'built of jasper' (v.18), its height and greatness speaking of perfect protection from all evil (v.27): see also Zechariah 2:5; John 10:28; Revelation 7:4; and other references to the city or wall of Jerusalem: *with twelve gates, and at the gates twelve angels,* do these represent the guardian angels of the tribes of Israel? *cf* Michael, the guardian archangel of the nation of Israel (Dan. 10:13, 21; 12:1); *and on the gates the names of the twelve tribes of the sons of Israel were inscribed;* [13]*on the east three gates, on the north three gates, on the south three gates, and on the west three gates.*

NB

Although the city of Jerusalem at the present time is more nearly four-square than ever, as a rocky crag its gates would always have opened to the four quarters of the compass, east, north, south, west. The best biblical accounts of the walls of Jerusalem are found in Ezekiel chapter 48 and Nehemiah chapter 3, and these may be compared with maps and suggested plans of the city in different ages as found in a Bible atlas. Such geography provides a fascinating study; and although much is speculative, modern archaeology helps.

The naming and order of the twelve tribes of Israel come from Ezekiel 48:30–35, which order (and that of the gates) is related to the ideal order of the apportioning of the land (Ezek. 48:1–8; 23–29). Note Ezekiel 48:30–35 that the spiritual order of the tribes is preserved: first, Leah's sons, Reuben, Judah, Levi; Rachel's sons, Joseph, Benjamin; and the son of Rachel's maid, Dan; Leah's other sons, Simeon, Issachar, Zebulun; and lastly, the sons of Leah's maid, Gad, Asher, and the son of Rachel's maid, Naphtali.

[14]*And the wall of the city had twelve foundations and on them the twelve names of the twelve apostles of the Lamb.* See

Matthew 19:28; Ephesians 2:20. Here, and at verse 12, we have the twelve tribes of Israel, and the twelve apostles of the Lamb, as the ground and foundation upon which the church is built, 'Christ Jesus himself being the cornerstone.' (Eph. 2:20; but see also 1 Cor. 3:11) This is what our Lord meant in His controversial statement in Matthew 16:18: 'And I tell you, you are Peter (*Petros*), and on this rock (*petra*) I will build my church. and the gates of hades shall not prevail against it.'

[15]*And he who talked to me had a measuring rod of gold to measure the city and its gates and walls.* Measure suggests definition, for the saints are a particular company, although innumerable to us ('The Lord knows those who are his'; 2 Tim. 2:19); see verse 27. [16]*The city lies foursquare, its length the same as its breadth; and he measured the city with his rod, twelve thousand stadia; its length and breadth and height are equal.* cf Solomon's 'perfect cube', 1 Kings 6:20; Ezekiel chapters 40—48.

[17]*He also measured its wall, a hundred and forty-four cubits* (1 cubit = approximately eighteen inches) *by a man's measure, that is, an angel's.* It would be ridiculous to read this like an architect's plan: it is the perfections suggested by the regular dimensions of the city which are important. Here there is ample scope for aesthetic imagination, not only concerning the perfect form of Christ's completed church, but also concerning the beauty and perfections of the divine mind. Sometimes men of imagination and scientific knowledge speak of the Almighty as the divine Architect or Mathematician, and we see here something of what they mean. But the divine powers, for all their infinite resource and range, are directed primarily towards the perfections of Christ's church: the saints are the chief of creation, and Christ's church the peculiar object of our God's desire. Wonderful!

[18]*The wall was built of jasper,* 'clear as crystal' (v.11), *while the city was pure gold, cf* verse 21, *clear as glass. cf* Revelation 4:6; 15:2. To finite minds the combination of solidity and transparency is remarkable, as also the supreme value and durability of gold. The idea of all being seen and known in the heavenly city is not easy for us, since there is

148 A Vision of Glory

so much that is furtive in our lives, and which we fear to expose. But what in heaven may not be fully known, will not be hid by darkness or impenetrable solidity, but by excess of light. 'The King of kings and Lord of lords...alone has immortality and dwells in unapproachable light, whom no man has ever seen or can see.' (1 Tim. 6:16)

[19]*The foundations of the wall of the city were adorned with every jewel;* see Isaiah 54:11–12. Although these stones may be compared with the twelve on the high priest's breastplate (Exod. 28:17–20; 39:10–13), we should note that accurate identification is not possible since there was no scientific terminology in Bible times (I. Howard Marshall, *The New Bible Dictionary,* article on jewels). The most intriguing knowledge here would be the indentification of the colour of each stone with its corresponding tribe of Israel.

Marc Chagall, the Russian Jewish artist, sought to portray this in stained glass windows in the synagogue of the Hadasa Hospital, Jerusalem. He derives the order of the tribes from Genesis 49, and his inspiration for the character portrayals of the sons of Jacob from the same source. The colours and scripture references for each are as follows: Reuben, blue, 'the first-born of Israel...unstable as water.' Simeon, blue 'Cursed by their anger, for it is fierce; and their wrath, for it is cruel!' Levi, yellow, 'They shall teach thy ordinances unto Jacob, and thy law unto Israel.' Judah, red, 'like a lion's whelp...the sceptre shall not depart from Judah.' Zebulun, red, 'shall dwell at the haven of the sea.' Issachar, green, 'is a strong ass couching down between two burdens.' Dan, blue, 'shall judge his people...a serpent by the way.' Gad, green, 'whom a troop shall overcome, but he shall overcome at the last.' Asher, green, 'More than all the children be Asher blessed...he shall bathe his foot in oil.' Naphtali, yellow, 'like a fleet hind.' Joseph, yellow, 'is a fruitful bough by a spring.' Benjamin, blue, 'The beloved of the Lord, he shall dwell in safety.'

The colours do not tell us much, since only four main colours are used, with little distinction in shades of the same colour. It is not possible to work out a correspondence between tribes and stones, because there are no clear

guiding lines from comparison of the various lists. Perhaps
it remains meantime a speculative study for Christian
aesthetes!

the first was jasper, surely, crystal clear (v.11), *the second
sapphire,* blue, the third agate, AV 'chalcedony', translucent
quartz, which may have been green, *the fourth emerald,*
green, but the LXX (Septuagint) for Exodus 28:18; 39:11;
Ezekiel 27:16 has 'anthrax', a burning coal, which may have
been red, [20]*the fifth onyx,* AV 'sardonyx', an agate, 'with
layers of brown and white' (Marshall), *the sixth carnelian,* or
sardius red, cf Revelation 4:3, *the seventh chrysolite,* yellow
topaz or quartz, *the eighth beryl,* green, *the ninth topaz,*
yellow, *the tenth chrysoprase,* apple green? *the eleventh
jacinth,* hyacinth blue, *the twelfth amethyst,* a 'purple variety
of transparent crystalline quartz' (Marshall).

Charles suggests from Josephus (Antiquities 3.7.7) and
Philo (Life of Moses 2.124–6) that the stones in the high
priest's breastplate were connected with the signs of the
zodiac. He gives a list which identifies the stones with the
signs, the order in which 'the sun passes through the
constellations' being the reverse of that in Revelation.
Suffice it that the stones represent a spectrum of colours
(both in Exodus 28:17–20 and in Revelation 21:19–20), and
that these are somehow intended to represent the various
characters of the twelve sons of Israel, and their tribes. This
is what Chagall is trying to do in his windows from
significant references to the respective sons of Jacob in
Genesis 49. A study of the prophetic element in these
references in relation to the subsequent history of the tribes,
and of important characters in them, proves fascinatingly
interesting, and valuable.

[21]*And the twelve gates were twelve pearls, each of the gates
made of a single pearl.* The twelve gates, three on each side
of the city, have the names of the twelve tribes of the sons of
Israel, which can only mean that the way into the celestial
city is by the twelve tribes of Israel as the repository of the
oracles of God; see Deuteronomy 4:8; Psalm 147:19; Romans
2:17–20; 3:2; 9:4. The beautiful lustre of the pearl reminds
of Christ, whose kingdom is the pearl of great price (Matt.
13:45), and those by whom entrance into the city is gained

naturally reflect the lustre of the kingdom and the beauty of the King. 'How beautiful upon the mountains are the feet of him who brings good tidings, who publishes peace, who brings good tidings of good, who publishes salvation, who says to Zion, "Your God reigns."' (Is. 52:7) There is also the thought of the complete and rounded beauty of the pearl. As the perfections of Christ are discovered to those who enter in and find Him, so His beauties come to be seen in those who attract others to Him by their lustre.

and the street of the city was pure gold, transparent as glass. Entrance having been gained, there is complete communication within, with fellowship between God and man of the most transparent sort. Nothing is dark, obscure, or hidden; all is known and understood, except, as we have said, what may be impenetrable by excess of light; see 1 Corinthians 13:12. This has to be weighed against the 'secret' of Revelation 2:17b, although perhaps the emphasis there is not upon the *secrecy*, but upon the uniqueness of each saint's fellowship with the Father, and his singular value to Him.

[22]*And I saw no temple in the city, for its temple is the Lord God the Almighty and the Lamb.* See 2 Samuel 7:1–16; 1 Kings 8:27, 30; Ephesians 2:22; Hebrews 3:3–6; 1 Peter 2:4–10. In these scriptures there is an interplay of the ideas of God dwelling in us and we in Him; see John 15:4–7; 17:23; Acts 17:24–29; Revelation 7:15; 21:3.

[23]*And the city has no need of sun or moon to shine upon it, for the glory of God is its light, and its lamp is the Lamb.* All is personal here, neither abstract nor sub-personal (light before lights, Gen. 1:3–5, 16–19); so that there is no need of astronomical, solar or lunar light (Acts 2:20); but all is spiritual and glorious! See Isaiah 60:20; John 1:1–9, 14; 8:12; Acts 26:13; 1 Timothy 6:16. Thomas Binney saw this:

> Eternal Light! eternal Light!
> How pure the soul must be,
> When placed within Thy searching sight,
> It shrinks not, but with calm delight,
> Can live, and look on Thee!

The spirits that surround Thy throne
May bear the burning bliss;
But that is surely theirs alone,
Since they have never, never known
A fallen world like this.

O how shall I, whose native sphere
is dark, whose mind is dim,
Before the Ineffable appear,
And on my naked spirit bear
The uncreated beam?

There is a way for man to rise
To that sublime abode:
An offering and a sacrifice,
A Holy Spirit's energies,
An Advocate with God.

These, these prepare us for the sight
Of holiness above:
The sons of ignorance and night
May dwell in the eternal Light,
Through the eternal Love!

²⁴*By its light shall the nations walk; and the kings of the earth shall bring their glory into it.* The anthropomorphism of these words, with those of verse 26, constrains us to regard them (and the passage from 21:1—22:5) as belonging to some future period of the present millennial, messianic, gospel age of Jesus Christ. It is a spiritual conception dressed in earthbound terms, but the absence of a temple, and the solar and lunar orbs surely convinces us that it is not descriptive of our natural, earthbound, mortal existence. ²⁵*and its gates shall never be shut by day—and there shall be no night there* (22:5); darkness is unthinkable (1 John 1:5) when the uncreated light of the eternal God fully manifests His glory: all the darkness will be banished to the nether regions, see Matthew 25:30; 2 Peter 2:17; Jude 13b; Revelation 16:10.

²⁶*they shall bring into it the glory and the honour of the nations.* This is not easy to understand: what can it mean but that the Gentile nations gladly submit to the supremacy

of Christ and enter the realm of the King of kings and Lord of lords? If this is so, it looks back to the promise which God gave to Abram (Gen. 12:3b), and renewed frequently during the Old Testament dispensation, *eg* in Isaiah 42:6; 49:6; see also Matthew 25:31–33; Romans 11:12, 15, 25; 15:9–16.

[27]*But nothing unclean shall enter it, nor any one who practises abomination or falsehood,* see the finality of the state after death in Revelation 22:11–12, and the fact of the great divide expressed in terms of 22:14–15; *but only those who are written in the Lamb's book of life. cf* also Revelation 13:8; 17:8; 20:12, 15. These are chosen in Christ from before the foundation of the world (Eph. 1:4), and are predestined to be His unto all eternity; but their eternal election is wrought out in terms of the response of saving faith to the effectual calling of sovereign grace.

"The fact of the great divide"

Thy Sovereign grace to all extent
Immense + unconfined
From age to age it never ends
It reaches all mankind.

CHAPTER TWENTY TWO

The New Eden
22:1–21

We now come to the second, last, and heavenly Eden.

¹*Then He showed me the river of the water of life, bright as crystal, flowing from the throne of God and of the Lamb* ²*through the middle of the street of the city*; Throughout Scripture, living (running) water (*eg* as rivers and streams) represents the life it sustains, both natural and spiritual. See Genesis 2:4–14; Exodus 17:6; Leviticus 14:52; Numbers 20:11; Psalm 46:4; Song of Solomon 4:15; Jeremiah 2:13, 17:13; Zechariah 14:8; John 4:7–15; Ezekiel 47:1–6 (but for the whole plan of the ideal Jerusalem, Ezekiel chs. 40–48 should be studied); John 7:37–39; Revelation 7:17; 22:17. Concerning the Lamb, compare 'the throne of God and of the Lamb' (and Rev. 3:21) with 'in the midst of the throne' (7:17); and also 5:6); *also, on either side of the river, the tree of life* (Gen. 2:9; 3:22, 24) *with its twelve kinds of fruit*, see Genesis 2:9, 16; 3:2; Jeremiah 17:8; Ezekiel 47:7, 12; see also Psalm 1:3; *yielding its fruit each month; and the leaves of the tree were for the healing of the nations.*

The idea of one tree yielding twelve kinds of fruit, one per month, is fantastic (*cf* Gal. 5:22, 23, where 'fruit' [nine items] is singular), and indicates the symbolical and spiritual nature of the picture, representing perpetual fruitfulness, and suggesting the paradisal or edenic nature of the blessings of eternal life.

What does the 'healing of the nations' mean in that idyllic situation? Hendriksen reminds us that the vision is ideal

153

(*More than Conquerors*, p112). There are, therefore, combined in the one picture, elements representing the perfection of the eternal state, and others representing heavenly blessings capable of enjoyment in a temporal condition of things.

The salvation of the nations is a theme which runs through the Scriptures, *eg* Genesis 12:3; Isaiah 42:6; 49:6; Matthew 25:32; Romans 11:11–15; 15:7–16; Ephesians 2:11—3:11. There is one term for 'Gentiles' in both Greek and Hebrew, although in biblical Hebrew the word means 'nation', and in rabbinic Hebrew 'non-Jew'; the term may therefore mean 'races' or 'peoples' in certain contexts, and merely non-Jews in others.

[3]*There shall no more be anything accursed, but the throne of God and of the Lamb shall be in it,* The banishment of evil is expressed in negative terms, since we live in a world which is dominated by what is wicked and accursed and, in the patience of God, not yet removed. The positive is expressed in terms of the throne and the reign of God and the Lamb, through Whom such a blessed prospect is ours. Nor is it a glossy and impersonal ideal, like a still photograph or a petrified city; we read of activity. *and his servants shall worship him*; this surely means that God's servants will find perfect forms by which to express their total and unending debt to God.

[4]*they shall see his face,* Set this over against Exodus 33:20, 23 (Exod. 33:11 should be understood differently). Nor ought we to be limited or confused by the plural in 'God and the Lamb', for, as on earth the face of Jesus Christ is virtually the face of the Father (John 14:9), so, in heaven, it will be in the face of Jesus Christ, the Lamb of God (still human, indeed for ever human!), that we shall see the face of the Father. Are we not helped to understand what this means when we say that we see the face of a father in his son? To the yearning soul the words, 'and they shall see his face', must be amongst the most beautiful and evocative in the Bible! *and his name shall be on their foreheads.* Not a written inscription on redeemed foreheads, both disfiguring and ridiculous, but the imprint or comely likeness of all that the blessed Name represents in the beauty and grace of the

person of Jesus Christ. The idea comes from the orthodox Jewish practice of placing tiny 'boxes' with inscribed passages of the Torah (Law) in the 'frontlets' of the eyes, see Exodus 13:16; Deuteronomy 6:8; 11:18. The vision points the contrast between such external witness to the truth (see Exod. 34:34–35), and the personified witness of a Christ-like, gracious bearing, see Jeremiah 31:33; John 1:14, 18; 14:9; Acts 6:15.

See the opposite of this image in, *eg* the leprous forehead (2 Chron. 26:19); the harlot's brow (Jer. 3:3); the mark of the beast (Rev. 14:9); and the name of mystery: 'Babylon the great, mother of harlots and of earth's abominations' (Rev. 17:5).

[5]*And night shall be no more*; this is hinted at in Zechariah 14:6–7; and see Revelation 21:23, 25; *they need no light of lamp or sun*, which must mean that the very possibility of darkness is excluded. A study of the references to darkness in Scripture is illuminating and suggestive, *eg* darkness as existing in the midst of primeval matter before the Fall (Gen. 1:2, 4, 5, 18); the depth of darkness of Egypt's night (Exod. 10;21). On the other hand, the darkness in which, Solomon declared, God dwelt, is surely the impenetrable darkness of light (1 Kings 8:12; also Ps. 18:9, 11). Job says profound things about darkness, natural and spiritual (*eg* 10:21–22). Psalm 139 makes plain that God dwells above and beyond both darkness and light (139:12): He creates them (Isa. 45:7). In the New Testament, darkness is, more uniformly, that which Christ came to dispel, *eg* Matthew 6:23; Luke 1:79; John 1:5; Acts 26:18; 2 Corinthians 4:6; Ephesians 5:5, 8; Colossians 1:13; 1 Peter 2:9: 'in him is no darkness at all' (1 John 1:5).

Whether we think of darkness as a natural creation, or as the dreadful spiritual reality emanating from the Almighty's abandoned creature, Satan, both are to be banished, so that the whole re-constituted universe will be light, with 'no darkness at all'. This is more than interesting in relation to the outshining of the glory of God in the face of Jesus Christ; for it suggests (21:23) that when the Creator of the universe has manifested His glory fully through Jesus Christ and His church, there will be no need even of the natural lights which He made to lighten the world. This is great and vast enough to tax our powers of thought and imagination. *for the Lord God will be their light, and they shall reign for ever and ever*. All these wonders are directly related to the saints.

⁶*And*, in the epilogue (6–21) which now follows, *he said to me, 'These words are trustworthy and true. And the Lord, the God of the spirits of the prophets, cf* 1 Corinthians 14:32–33; Revelation 1:1–3; 19:10, *has sent his angel to show his servants what must soon take place.'* Here again we have the transmission of the Revelation from the Lord to His angel and thence to His servants (*cf* 1:1–3). The significance of the strange phrase, 'the God of the spirits of the prophets' (*cf* 1 Cor. 14:32, 33), is the divine control of all agents, angelic and human. The personal note in verse 7, *'And behold, I am coming soon'*, shows that it is the Lord Christ who is in command and is speaking. The note concerning the imminence of the Lord's coming is the thread which runs through these diverse final observations.

As to the imminence of the coming, T. F. Torrance says, 'The New Testament does not think of the difference between the presence of Christ here and now and His Second Advent so much in terms of a passage of time as the difference between the veiled and the unveiled. That is why the whole of the New Testament by an inner necessity of personal faith thinks of that day as imminent. The pressure of that imminence may be so great upon the mind as to turn the thin veil of sense and time into apocalyptic imagery behind which it is given to see the consummation of all things.' (*The Apocalypse Today*, p.186)

⁷*Blessed is he who keeps the word' of the prophecy of this book*. The importance of the word 'prophecy' here is that the sum of the message of the Revelation—that Christ is coming soon—is prophetic to all who heed it, and that all things revealed in the book are the accompaniments of His coming, before, during and after. The stress is on the blessing to those who receive it, and who frame their lives accordingly.

The wonder is, as with all Scripture divinely revealed and inspired but humanly mediated, that it came through a

human mind. *⁸I John am he who heard and saw these things.*
But not in the ordinary course of daily life, but pheno-
menally; *cf* Moses (Exod. 3), Isaiah (Is. 6), Daniel (Dan. 10),
Paul (2 Cor. 12), and John (Rev. 1). *And when I heard and
saw them, I fell down to worship at the feet of the angel who
showed them to me*; *cf* Revelation 19:9–10, and notes
thereon; *⁹but he said to me, 'You must not do that! I am a
fellow servant with you and your brethren the prophets, and
with,* note how those who succeed the apostles and prophets
are described, *those who keep the words of this book. Worship
God.'* A practical word here: the worship of God ought to be
so pure that it transcends all spiritistic phenomena. There
are escapist dangers, doubtless, in the contemplation of the
mystics, but there is, none the less, a contemplation of our
divine Maker and God which is life, health and peace,
because it ministers salvation.

*¹⁰And he said to me, 'Do not seal up the words of the
prophecy of this book, for the time is near.'* This is a distinctly
different command from that given to other inspired men; *eg*
Isaiah (Is. 8:16), Daniel (Dan. 8:26; 12:4, 9); or different from
Paul's reaction (2 Cor. 12:4). The attitude which omits the
book of the Revelation from even a systematic ministry of
the Word because it is full of mystery and difficulties is
inexcusable in the light of the urgency of its final section.

*¹¹'Let the evildoer still do evil, and the filthy still be filthy,
and the righteous still do right, and the holy still be holy.'* The
urgency arises from the finality of the division of mankind
consequent upon Christ's coming. Although there are two
descriptions of both categories here, the evildoer and the
filthy, the righteous and the holy, the stress is on radical
division, as also on the permanency of the states described.
That is to say, the division of mankind at the final judgment
is not arbitrary, as if it depended upon some mere 'decision'
or confession made. Rather, the division is made according
to character, apparent to the all-seeing eye of God.
Character is the sum of the decisions and the consequent
actions of a lifetime. See Revelation 9:21; 16:9, 11, 21. This
is brought out in the next verse. *¹²'Behold, I am coming soon,
bringing my recompense, to repay every one for what has been
done.* The sweeping finality of this judgment is indicated by

what follows: *[13]I am the Alpha and the Omega, cf* 1:8 *the first and the last, the beginning and the end.'* The doctrine of reward or loss for believers is fully documented in the New Testament; see 1 Corinthians 3:10–15; 2 Corinthians 5:10; Revelation 19:8.

[14]Blessed are those who wash their robes, see Psalm 51:2, 7; Isaiah 1:16; 4:4; Ephesians 5:26, 27; Revelation 1:5; 7:14; *that they may have the right to the tree of life,* see verse 2 and Genesis 2:9; 3:22, 24, *and that they may enter the city by the gates.* What does John mean by 'that they may enter the city by the gates'? Is he stressing the proper (and only possible) entrance, as in John 10:1–3? Or is the emphasis upon the gates as in 21:12, 21, with 'the names of the twelve tribes of the sons of Israel' inscribed on them? There is no salvation outside Christ's church!

[15]Outside are the dogs (Ps. 22:16, 20; Phil. 3:2) *and sorcerers* (Exodus. 7:11; Deut. 18:9–14; Dan. 2:2; Mal. 3:5; Acts 8:9–11; Rev. 9:21; 18:23; 21:8) *and fornicators and murderers* (see on 21:8) *and idolators, and every one who loves and practises falsehood.* The last category, lovers and practitioners of falsehood, are those who, beguiled by Satan, are at last completely sold to his ways and possessed by his prime motive, deceit, as the only way possible in God's world to seduce men from Him.

[16]'I Jesus have sent my angel to you with this testimony for the churches. I am the root and the offspring of *David, the bright morning star.'* See, again, notwithstanding the angelic presence, the authoritative and commanding presence of the Lord Himself. See also His association with the history of redemption, as rooted in David; yet He is the cosmic Christ. *Cf* Numbers 24:15–17; Isaiah 11:1; and Jesus' riddle (Ps. 110.1, and Matt. 22:41–46).

[17]The Spirit and the Bride say, 'Come.' The church, inspired by the Holy Spirit, echoes the Spirit's wooing note to the Lord whom she has learned to love—and longs for. *And let him who hears say, 'Come.'* To long for Christ and His coming is here the mark of the Christian not only convinced, but captivated by love of Christ, a sign of maturity in the things of the Spirit. *And let him who is thirsty come, and let him who desires take the water of life*

(Is. 55:1a; John 6:35; 7:37–39; Rev. 22:1) *without price* (Is. 55:1b; Rom. 3:24; 5:15–17).

[18]*I warn every one who hears the words of the prophecy of this book: if any one adds to them, God will add to him the plagues described in this book*, Not unnaturally, this warning was issued to Israel upon the giving of the Law, see Deuteronomy 4:2; 12:32. We find such a warning also in the words of Agur in Proverbs 30:5–6: 'Every word of God (having been smelted) proves true; he is a shield to those who take refuge in him. Do not add to his words, lest he rebuke you, and you be found a liar.'

[19]*and if any one takes away from the words of the book of this prophecy, God will take away his share in the tree of life and in the holy city, which are described in this book*. See Jeremiah 26:2; Ezekiel 2:8—3:21; 1 Enoch 104:10–11. Charles says, 'A terrible judgment is foretold (2 Enoch 48:7–8) for those who tamper with the words of this book.' *(International Critical Commentary, p.223)*

Morris reminds us of the same concern expressed in respect of the translation of the LXX or Septuagint (the third century BC translation of the Old Testament into Greek) in the Letter of Aristas. When the Greek translation of the Old Testament was completed, 'they bade them pronounce a curse in accordance with their custom upon any who should make any alteration either by adding anything or changing in any way whatever any of the words which had been written or making an omission. This was a very wise precaution to ensure that the book might be preserved for all the future time unchanged.' (Morris, *Revelation*, p.262)

The severity of the warnings should be noted, both against the positive sin of commission, with its positive threat of plagues, and the negative sin of omission with its negative threat of the loss of the tree of life and entrance into the holy city: these are complementary.

Futhermore, while the reference in these two verses is clearly to the book of the Revelation, those who believe the Bible to be the very Word of God, fully inspired, accept the whole canon of Scripture as coming under these strictures, and fear to tamper with any part of the sacred volume. See

Isaiah 40:8; Matthew 5:17–20; 24:35. 'Heaven and earth will pass away, but my words will not pass away.'

[20]*He who testifies to these things says, 'Surely I am coming soon.' Amen. Come, Lord Jesus!*

In the spirit of response to this blessed promise this interim study has been undertaken and revised. It ends with the prayer that those who read the book of Revelation may also respond, and add their cry to that of those who long for the Lord to hasten His coming.

[21]*The grace of the Lord Jesus be with all the saints. Amen.*